THE THIRD GOD

Predictions and Challenges
for the next Millenium

THE THIRD GOD

Predictions and Challenges
for the next Millenium

So Namoo

Rutledge Books, Inc.

Danbury, CT

Rutledge Books, Inc.
107 Mill Plain Road, Danbury, CT 06811
1-800-278-8533
www.rutledgebooks.com

Manufactured in the United States of America

Cataloging in Publication Data
Namoo, So
  The third god
  ISBN: 1-58244-009-3
  1. Peace. 2. Philosophy.
299/.5142

CONTENTS

Prologue

We are inevitably heading towards a new century and a completely different millennium in a couple of years.

In retrospect, the twentieth century was a very turbulent and unpredictable century. There are many examples of the nearly miraculous changes and hardships that occurred during the twentieth century. Early in the twentieth century, the Great Depression upset national economies throughout the world, and millions of people suffered from chronic unemployment. Humankind had two major world wars that wrought tremendous destruction across the globe, and for the first time in human history and in the same century, we sent satellites into space and began an era of exploration beyond the confines of our planet. Two atomic bombs dropped on Hiroshima and Nagasaki and annihilated thousands of Japanese civilians in the blink of an eye and left their charred remains under pitch-black radioactive ashes. The disastrous leak in the Soviet nuclear power plant at Chernobyl exposed the unsuspecting natural world to perilous radioactive substances; even now, we do not know the dire consequences that will result from the contamination of the environment from these radioactive substances. We also were able to land on the moon and explore the moon's surface for the first time in history; in previous centuries, no one would have dared to imagine travel in space and on the moon.

The next century will probably be even more tumultuous than the twentieth century. Who knows what obscure fate the future has in store for humanity as a whole? We have no clear idea how the future will change; we have no conception of how the next century will be different from this one, just like people who lived in previous centuries.

Especially since humanity is entering into a new millennium with critical problems, such as the current population explosion, overcrowding, environmental pollution, destruction of nature at an unimaginable pace, a widespread collapse of moral and ethical values in the family and society, a polarization between rich and poor, and conflict between different religious beliefs, humankind feels uneasy and anxious about the resolution of these difficulties in the future. How will we survive the coming millennium and what knowledge will we need to survive?

The ship named earth, with six billion passengers of Homo sapiens and billions of natural species on board, is heading for very murky, foggy, rough, and stormy seas. Nobody knows whether the ship will sink and fade into oblivion or learn to survive the hazardous weather of the coming millennium.

There are thousands of books that express future visions and predictions concerning how the next century will be a period of turbulent change that will demand solutions to the problems plaguing humanity. There are essentially three major types of visions for the next century in the majority of these books.

The first type of vision states that democracy will prevail all over the world, and human rights will improve throughout the globe. Science and technology will develop faster and become more efficient, and trade between nations will increase as a result. Everyone will live a more convenient, economically prosperous, and peaceful lifestyle. There will be no lethal battles nor deadly nuclear holocausts that will jeopardize the well-being of humanity as in the chaotic twentieth century.

The second type of vision asserts that Asian countries will become stronger in the military and economic sectors and will become more competitive with the rest of the world. The center of civilization will move to Asia and inaugurate an Asian era. This theory has already been disproven by the collapse of the Asian economy in the global marketplace.

The third vision describes the contours of a global catastrophe of untold proportions: rampant crime, increased poverty, drugs, violence, excessive consumption of the world's resources, nuclear warfare, the inevitable destruction of nature, and the fateful exinction of human beings from the face of the earth. Not a single soul will live after humanity annihilates itself, and perhaps all that lives in the natural world will perish.

All of these visions of the next century are mostly influenced by a Western philosophy and worldview. Even the predictions coming from Asian leaders and scholars cannot avoid being influenced by the Western perception of the world, especially since the West is the center of twentieth-century global civilization.

My vision of the future is different from these predictions because it is mostly based on Eastern thought and philosophy concerning the changes in the coming millennium. These three types of predictions have failed to foretell the three most significant changes in the future.

The paradigm will shift.

The paradigm is the natural foundation for the life of humanity and the natural species existing on earth.

God will change.

Democracy will change.

When the paradigm changes, everything changes.

How could one survive into the next millennium without gathering the proper information in order to prepare for the inevitable transformation in paradigm? Without the critical knowledge concerning the coming unavoidable paradigm change, a person's view is narrowly restricted to the present and blind to changes in the future, like the summer locust that fails to anticipate winter and dies as a result of its own blindness. Entire species perish because they did not have the information necessary to survive when the environment changed, and Homo sapiens, which is also subject to the natural laws of the universe, is no exception to the law of evolution.

Now, in the twentieth century, we are living in the vertical paradigm; the vertical paradigm is a hierarchical paradigm with the ruling classes dominating the ruled. In the next century, the paradigm will naturally evolve into a horizontal paradigm where distinctions between ruler and ruled will no longer exist as in the past. This change may appear improbable from the perspective of the people living in our present vertical society, but changes have already begun to occur as human rights issues and environmental issues become more important for people from different cultures and backgrounds around the world. People have gained more information about the devastating effects of racism, ethnic cleansing, and genocide, as well as the massive destruction of the environment. Every day, on the television and in the newspaper, they can read about the devastating effects of poverty and material inequalities in the world. Naturally, as people become more educated, they will desire to change their situation and minimize the amount of suffering and intolerance in the world. They will not be able to improve their situation all at once, and it will take time for the human species to evolve beyond its present ignorance and present inequalities, but change will occur.

I will explain how the paradigm will shift.

In order to survive in the next century and the coming millennium, people will have to adapt to the paradigm and learn about the different paradigm while updating and discarding previous beliefs. The old beliefs that our ancestors have had and the present beliefs that many people have will no longer be valuable in the future because the cultural, intellectual, and moral landscape of the peoples of the world will rapidly change in the coming millennium.

PARADIGM

Change is the eternal law of the universe.

Daytime changes into nighttime, cold seasons change into hot seasons, younger generations replace older generations, birth changes into death, and everything that lives in the universe constantly evolves or becomes extinct. There is simply no end or beginning to this process as far as the limited experience and imagination of humankind can perceive.

The most significant change we can imagine concerns the beginning of life in the ocean and its subsequent evolution into terrestrial life on land. Finally, the highest form of mammals evolved into Homo sapiens. As human beings continue to evolve, adaptation to life in space will also be possible. On the universal scale, there might be more important changes occurring, but our limited imagination and intelligence cannot easily grasp the meaning of these changes.

On earth, there are periodic cycles of change that we call seasons, such as spring, summer, autumn, and winter, and these cycles change in a three-month period. In different parts of the earth, seasons change earlier, while some parts change later. Some parts of the earth change for a long time, and in some places, the changes occur for a shorter period of time. In some parts of the earth, such as the

North Pole and the South Pole, which remain cold throughout the year, as well as the equator, which remains warm throughout the year, the weather does not change as much. But most of the earth's climate changes seasonally in a three-month period.

Although the cycle of the seasons happens once every year on earth, other cycles in the natural world, such as the natural life span of different species, can be much briefer or last many years. Insects, such as butterflies and mosquitoes, have relatively short life cycles-many live just a few weeks and others die after only a few days-while the locust appears just once every seven years. Most larger animals have longer life spans, ranging from a year or two for rodents, 10 years and longer for dogs and cats, and upwards to parrots and elephants that can live 50 years or more. The upper limit for humans is over 100 years, yet in the past, few people have reached this age due to limited medical resources, warfare, disease, and malnourishment.

But there are other, more subtle cycles beyond our basic life cycles. Mankind as an entity and an evolving civilized species also has a cycle that has a defined and predictable beginning, middle, and end. While the life cycles of insects are measured in months and those for people in years, civilized humanity's cycle of change is measured in millennia.

Approximately every three thousand years, humankind undergoes a dramatic paradigm shift that results in a complete change in human attitudes and behavior, a change which facilitates emotional, intellectual, and spiritual advancement. Without this impressive change, civilization would never have developed nor would the advances that have pushed humankind to ever greater technological, spiritual, and economic improvements have ever occurred.

The three-month cycles of change in the natural world are known as seasons, and the 100-year cycle of Homo sapiens is known as a life span. But what do we call humankind's slow moving evolution and shifting paradigm that happens so gradually that few people con-template its occurrence? Humankind's three-thousand-year cycle of change is called *kunmady*.

What makes a human being different from other species? Before we discuss the changes in human society, we have to show how Homo sapiens differ from other species. While nobody knows the exact date when the first Homo sapiens first appeared on earth, the oldest fossils on record date back to 400,000 years, a time that pre-cedes the dawn of toolmaking. Prehistoric humans were cave dwellers who roamed the earth in a constant quest for food, and although they possessed the ability to speak, there was minimal social structure and no written language. Even so, archaeologists and anthropologists have been able to glean a decent amount of information about the lifestyle and activities of our distant ancestors from ancient bones and tool remnants.

But an even more profound question, which cannot be answered from the unearthed artifacts and skeletal remains of prehistoric humans, remains to be resolved. What truly separates Homo sapi-ens from the rest of the animal kingdom and elevates humankind above other animals as the most intelligent form of life?

In general scientific terms, we know that our species' large brain plus the combined ability to walk erect and to communicate by speech classifies us as human, but on a more profound level, what makes us complete human beings? Some anthropologists claim that the definitive moment when Homo sapiens distinguished itself from other species in the natural world occurred when our ancestors developed the ability to use fire.

Scientists suppose that our prehistoric ancestors learned about fire from trees set ablaze by bolts of lightning or from spouting vol-canic eruptions, and then they carefully kept fires burning in huts or caves. By harnessing the power of fire, they were able to cook their food, so it was easier to eat and tasted better. By the light of torches, humans could find their way more easily in the darkness.

Fire protected them from wild beasts, and they could improve their wooden tools by hardening the points with fire.

With fire to keep them warm in freezing weather, they could live in colder regions and spread across the earth from tropical regions to areas with seasonal climates. By learning to make fire and use fire to improve the quality of their life, our early ancestors learned that knowledge of the natural world could improve their lives for the future.

Other researchers suggest that early humans set the stage for modern civilization with the development of tools made for specific purposes. The first tools used by humans were clubs, digging sticks, stone hammers and knives, all of which were extensions of the original tool and weapon-the hand. Eventually, human beings created better tools, some of which became weapons. The spear and the bow and arrow turned men into more successful hunters and enhanced the quality of their lives.

As game became easier to hunt, humans settled down in small communities and out of the desire to grow their own crops, the plow was invented. Because of this invention, human beings could cultivate the land and harvest more and better food. Ultimately, Homo sapiens evolved from a hunting and gathering mode of subsistence to an agrarian one, which in turn facilitated the formation of increasingly larger communities.

Homo sapiens are not the only species on the earth that use tools. Chimpanzees use stones and clubs to crack nuts and to take fruit from trees, and some birds use small stones to crack eggs and make nests with twigs.

The original tools used by humankind were clubs and stones and resembled the tools used by other species. When humans invented the bow, humans developed a technology that did not exist for other species. The bow is a sign of intelligence because, unlike simpler tools, the bow uses tension and a dynamic play of forces in order to send arrows towards its target.

With the invention of the bow and the arrow, human society progressed from a gathering society to a hunting society. With the bow, humans could capture larger animals; therefore, more people began to live together in communities. Families joined together and formed kinship groups, which produced new social groups. They moved around together in order to get food and sustain their communities, but they settled down in places where food was plentiful. They made those places their territory, and if they met other people, they would attack them to protect their territory.

Stronger groups attacked weaker groups while often killing some of them, capturing some of them, and sacrificing some of them to their gods. Some of the conquered became members of the stronger communities. The weaker village disappeared, and the stronger group became larger after the stronger group defeated the weaker village. The stronger community increased in numbers, gained more territory, and attacked more smaller villages. Eventually, all the small, less powerful villages simply disappeared from the land, and the stronger community built one huge community.

Hunting society is like a society of fish. If fish live in a tank without a food supply, then the strongest fish will eat the smaller fish whole and, eventually, the overpowering fish will swallow every fish it can consume in the tank. People in hunting societies are more intelligent than fish, but their behavior is still like fish.

The paradigm for hunting societies is a point paradigm, and according to the point paradigm, one point takes over the other points and becomes a larger point. Eventually, the small points disappear from the land, and there remains only one large point, like the large fish in the water tank.

A good example of the point paradigm society is the role of Rome and Carthage in history. When Rome attacked Carthage, almost all the people in Carthage, around 50,000 inhabitants, were slaughtered and enslaved, and the Romans looted all their possessions. They burned down and razed the whole village. They made it impossible for people to farm by scattering salt on the land, which prevented food from growing. Carthage vanished completely from the map, and the Roman Empire swallowed Carthage and became a bigger spot. Like the giant fish in the tank, there was no other point to consume. Like the last fish in the tank, the Roman Empire collapsed.

Hunting society, based on the point paradigm, is a society in the *first kunmady*.

About three thousand years after hunting society invented the bow, the first plow was invented in order to cultivate land and grow crops. The invention of the plow signaled the beginning of agrarian society. In order to produce more food, people had to cultivate the arable land more and more. In order to find more land, they had to conquer other people and take their territory. The more powerful groups captured the people who owned other lands and stole their land from them. But, this time, they did not kill or sacrifice on altars the conquered as people in the first kunmady did. They were more civilized and intelligent than people in the first kunmady because they used the conquered as slaves, or tenants, or as colonized people to cultivate crops.

Conquerors became high class, the conquered became low class, and class society began with the relationship between weaker and stronger and between richer and poorer. The formation of class began the vertical paradigm of society, and under the vertical paradigm, stronger nations politically dominate weaker nations and make them a colony while controlling the populace of the weaker nation for their own advantage. The horizontal paradigm that will develop in the future will transform relationships that are now unequal into a more egalitarian and harmonious relationship than ever before. It may be difficult to imagine this transformation in the present stage, but the beginning of a new horizontal society is already in progress as more groups of people form into different agencies and organizations to protect the rights of human beings and the environment.

Industrial society started a couple hundred years ago and is a continuation of the vertical paradigm; therefore, industrial society is an extension of the same vertical paradigm that served as the dominant model for agrarian society. The bourgeois that have more money, more property and a business became high class, and people who have no money and no business became low class. Instead of strong nations colonizing weaker nations, larger corporations presently attack the market of smaller corporations and practice economic conquest. In the vertical paradigm, the people who have less technical knowledge and cunning serve the more powerful and intelligent individuals who hold them under their control by denying them access to quality education, health care, equal representation, and material resources necessary for well-being.

In nature, if the air is cold and it is wintertime, nobody can escape from the cold air, and in the present world, nobody can escape living in the vertical paradigm. Whether one lives in Western society or in Eastern society, whether one lives in a democratic society or in a communist society, regardless of one's profession, one must live in a vertical society. No one can avoid living in a class society with an upper and lower class because such a society does not exist. Rich and stronger classes stay above lower classes, and poorer and weaker people stay at the bottom of society while toiling for the enrichment of the upper class.

As vertical society develops, the stronger and richer have more and more people under them. The stronger and more powerful become more developed, and the lower classes have to support more and more the needs of the ruling classes. Like a high-rise building, the top floor must be supported by all the lower floors, and the people who live at the top floor are living luxurious lives while the people below are struggling to support them. Then, the building becomes higher and higher from two hundred to three hundred stories until the people in the basement can no longer support the building. Therefore, the building will eventually collapse without a strong foundation.

People in vertical society are very intelligent, but their mind and behavior is much like the behavior of an untamed animal, and in the animal kingdom, the stronger species always conquer the weaker species.

The vertical paradigm society is the framework for the *second kunmady*.

About twenty-five years ago, human beings invented a new tool: the computer. The previous tools humankind invented, such as bows, plows, guns, paper, the wheel, the automobile, and the airplane, supplement the human body. For example, short legs cannot travel long distances, so trains, automobiles, and airplanes were invented. Trucks supplement the human back, since we are not able to carry heavy burdens. The cannon supplements the arm because it can throw projectiles further than the human arm. Computers supplement the human brain because the brain cannot collect so much information. The human brain is very limited and cannot make huge calculations and collect vast amounts of information, but the computer can store great amounts of information and make large calculations quickly.

But other tools must be operated by man at the scene, and for this reason, computers are different from other tools. Computers can operate on their own and continue to process information after receiving programming instructions, while other tools cannot operate on their own. The computer will help human beings develop a higher and more evolved consciousness in the next millennium and will promote the creation of a global society based on harmony.

When a computer controls a robot and can have parts similar to human body parts, the computer will act as the human brain. As a combination between computers and robots, a computerized robot will be able to perform any activity humans can do, and perhaps even with greater efficiency and intelligence. But computers will never be able to show emotion as human beings do.

With the present invention of this new and unique epochal and revolutionary tool, humankind will have entered a new society.

In the next society in the twenty-first century, which is called the information society, working with information will be the means of livelihood and will be the main industry of society. We will acquire more information and as we develop greater knowledge about ourselves and the world, we will wish to create a more harmonious society for the future.

In the first kunmady, most people worked with the bow, and in agrarian society, most people worked with the plow, and people in an information society presently work with the computer.

In the computer world, people work in cyberspace where there is no territory and no land-cyberspace is a boundless, unlimited world that does not exist on a map. No one can eliminate and sacrifice people in cyberworld, and no one can conquer people in cyberworld as in the past.

Most people work with computers independently. Unlike in the farm, where the supervisor watches over the toiling laborers and forces the laborer to work more, in cyberspace, no hard labor can happen. In the factory, supervisors who order the workers and push them to work harder cannot do that anymore. The people who work in the information industry, whether employer or employee, whether employed in a small company or a large corporation, possess more equality and more freedom from authority and from pressure than ever before.

There is virtually no oppression in cyberspace, and almost everyone is an independent part of cyberspace and the freedom it represents. No one can tell someone what to do in cyberspace, and one must have harmonious and productive relationships with other people in order to succeed. In cyberspace, people possess an almost equal level of freedom, rights, and commitment because they have no supervisor as in the past. With the advent of the information industry, the paradigm begins to change from the vertical to the horizontal. The horizontal society will be a far more equal and fair society than ever imagined before in previous history. This book will describe in detail in future chapters the implications of a new society — a society previous generations could not possibly imagine without the aid of the computer-and the improved quality of life.

In the next century, we will live in a horizontal society, and this paradigm will inevitably replace the vertical paradigm as a consequence of the information age. This horizontal society may not be easily imaginable now, but it is already beginning to develop with our modern communications systems and advanced computer networks.

GOD

Another unique characteristic that other species lack is awareness of God; God is the most omnipotent force that created everything within the universe. The importance of humankind's long-standing belief in God cannot be overstated because this belief has played a critical role in shaping public attitudes and behavior throughout human history.

At the dawn of civilization, people were completely dependent on the natural world to survive. They were also completely vulnerable to its rages-violent storms, earthquakes, and widespread plagues often threatened the human species with extinction. Because nature was such an all-encompassing power that appeared to control human destiny, and because people were ignorant about the laws of the natural world, it is easy to understand how the belief that God was nature developed. Without the help of scientific knowledge, they had no choice but to believe in God to explain the mysteries of the universe, both frightening and beautiful. Even now, some physicists and scientists admit that there is much that the human species cannot know and they acknowledge that there must be the existence of some supreme being that created the universe.

When early man watched the first buds forming on a tree, he

concluded that there must be some miracle happening in the tree causing the tree to grow. When herds of animals appeared every spring and came out of nowhere, it made sense to early humans that the mountain had produced these animals. The only explanation for the way the sun traveled across the sky, day in and day out, was that some divine force within the sun made the sun move every day.

After the winter was over and the warm winds of spring began to blow, a little green twig would sprout on trees. The little twigs would grow into branches which would eventually bear beautiful and delicious fruit-a process nothing short of miraculous to early man. Because of his extremely limited knowledge about the inner workings of nature, early man explained the inexplicable the only way that made sense to him-there must be a God living in the tree to cause it to bloom.

The same logic was used when explaining other mysteries of the natural world, which led to all sorts of nature divinities, including mountain gods, river gods, and thunder gods. The strongest of all was the sun god, which rules over the most powerful and successful civilizations of the first kunmady: Egyptian, Incan, and Mayan civilizations.

The interpretation of God's will as represented by the sun god and the other nature gods of early man is called *the first God*.

The paradigm of the first god was based on the belief that nature was important above all else because nature was divine. As a result, societies adopted what are now considered to be rather barbaric codes of ethics and behavior, such as the practice of human sacrifice, during which people were killed as part of a ritualistic religious offering or gift to the natural gods. Cannibalism was not uncommon; after they sacrificed human beings, priests and shamans consumed the flesh of the victims on the altars.

In an effort to appease the mighty nature gods, who controlled the weather and the crops and, therefore, man's very life in the first kunmady, temples and shrines were erected. Each temple was larger and more elaborate than the last. There usually were not enough citizens available to help out during construction, so in order to assemble the massive amount of manpower necessary for such a construction, slavery became an acceptable method to help increase the labor force and build giant temples.

Because humankind's intelligence evolved, the plow was invented. So, agrarian society began with the invention of the plow. People could cultivate crops, and as a result, they could produce their own food. They caught wild animals and domesticated them as livestock by putting them on pastures to graze, and they used cattle and sheep for food, clothes, and labor. Humans depended less on the whims of the natural world and depended instead on each other's labor to survive.

From this time on, people became suspicious about the old beliefs in the nature God, and they began to believe that human beings were superior to nature. The belief that human beings were superior to nature led to the present destruction of the environment that we are now witnessing in the modern world.

About three thousand years ago, in the foothills of the Himalayas, Buddha was born. He pointed one finger towards the heavens and one finger towards the earth, and said, "Man is the most superior being under the heavens and on earth."

Several centuries later, in the Middle East, Jesus Christ was born, and he said, "I am the only child of God." The meaning of this statement is: man only is God's child, and other species are consequently inferior in the eyes of man and God.

Centuries later, Mohammed appeared in the desert in the Middle East, and he said that he had heard a message from God through the angel Gabriel in human language.

All of these messages in different geographical areas and in different cultures might be different on the surface, but they all emphasize a single, very significant idea: man is the most superior species on earth and no other species is privileged enough to understand and interpret God's will.

These Gods for man only are called *the second Gods*, and the second kunmady begins at this time. This is the beginning of a new age that altered human history from the previous beliefs in the Nature god and from the barbaric rituals of cannibalism and human sacrifice, *the man first era*.

There are many other people who have communicated the same idea, i.e. man is superior to nature, but they did not reach as many people, while Buddha, Jesus Christ, and Mohammed's message spread across the entire world and reached nearly every human being on the planet.

People were very excited about Buddha, Jesus Christ, and Mohammed's message that man was the most divine, superior, and miraculous species on earth because they had lived under the terrible first God that demanded bloody sacrifices to nature.

People started to chop down trees, which were revered under the first God of nature. They built houses, schools and other facilities by chopping down trees, and they felt comfortable in their belief that man was superior to nature.

In order to harvest wheat, they burned down forests and mountains, which were worshipped as forest gods and mountain gods under the first kunmady.

They used rivers to build banks to irrigate the land.

Then, they built dams on the rivers that were once revered as river gods in the first kunmady in order to produce electricity.

During the second kunmady, humankind kept conquering nature for thousands of years and destroyed nature without mercy in the name of cultivation, development, and civilization.

People during the second kunmady took the senseless destruction of land and nature for granted because they felt it was their unique right and privilege as the unique children of God towering above the natural world.

Now, the natural world is in the process of being destroyed by humankind because of the rapid rate of development. Cities are rapidly replacing forests all across the world, and smog continually pollutes the atmosphere from urban traffic. The ozone in the ozone layer is rapidly disappearing, and ultraviolet rays are threatening the existence of many natural species daily. Thousands of species are disappearing from the face of the earth as humanity continues to conquer nature and destroy the natural environment, yet the destruction continues in spite of all the harm that has been done to nature. Species are dying on mountains, in tropical rain forests, in deserts, in rivers, in oceans, and virtually every corner of the earth is being destroyed every day. Acid rain and oil spills are also polluting the water and killing off many species of marine life.

Many species of birds, fish, reptiles, plants, trees, insects, and mammals are dying out rapidly and are on the verge of extinction. This is the same phenomenon that occurred in the last part of the first kunmady.

Because of the nature gods, many villages and many tribes disappeared as a result of the human sacrifices and slave labor necessary to build the altars of the God of nature. Sacrificing human beings to the nature gods at the end of the first kunmady is not so different from brutally destroying nature in the present time.

Because the second God's message states that human beings should master nature, people started to suspect that the second God's message had led to the destruction of many species on the earth and began to doubt that humankind should be above nature. Some people even denied that the second God's message was true and did not believe that humankind had the right to dominate nature and all of the species on the planet.

The second God's messages, which were written in bibles, i.e. the Buddhist bible, the Christian Bible, and the Koran, contradict much of the information, knowledge, and common sense acquired by people living in modern society.

Buddha said that a man who would meditate diligently with an open heart and open mind would get enlightened, and then the man would know all the truth in the world. The Buddha also said that humans could know where they came from and where they will go after this life, and how the world is formed and functions if they were enlightened.

But unfortunately, neither Buddha nor his followers who meditated years and years have found the two most important truths about the world: this planet is not flat, but round and spinning around the sun, and man was created by the earth because of evolution.

The Christian Bible states: the world was created in six days. Man was created like God, with dirt. Eve was made from Adam's rib. The first woman came from man. But modern science has proven with solid scientific evidence that man was created by the earth from evolution.

Allah commanded that his believers should not eat pork. Also, at the end of this world, everyone dead will come out of their tombs and will have the same appearance as before they died. Everyone will be judged before God-of course, the good guys will go to Eden and the bad guys will rot in hell. Eden resembles a rich man's dream-in paradise, there are many beautiful women, gold, and luxuries that cannot be acquired on earth.

These messages are unbelievable and disagreeable for modern people who have evolved since the coming of the second Gods and who are much more civilized, more knowledgeable, and more educated than the people of two thousand years ago. The ideas of the second Gods contradict and even reject modern scientific knowledge and technology.

People are rapidly losing faith in the second Gods.

According to statistics, two hundred years ago, almost everybody in the United States went to church every Sunday and believed in the second God. Now, less than 10 percent of people regularly go to church, and people with a higher education and the younger generation attend church less regularly. The media states that 50,000 Catholic priests left churches in the last decade, and the Catholic Church now lacks priests and is searching for priests from the younger generation.

Some churches, in order to attract more members, provided communities with services such as day care for young children of working families, health clubs, martial arts, and even rock bands. One church set up a bar to recruit more members, especially from the younger generation-one newspaper reported this surprising change.

On the earth, new, fresh cycles are beginning, and the man first paradigm is withering away. The second Gods, Gods of man, are vanishing with the man first paradigm, just as three thousand years ago, when the nature first paradigm ended while being replaced by the man first paradigm. What type of changes are occurring and how will humankind evolve in the future?

With the computer, an information society began and a horizontal paradigm will prevail in society and across the earth. Humankind will find a new God which will meet the demands of the new horizontal paradigm.

This God will not only exist for nature, like the first God, and, furthermore, will not be a God for only man, like the second Gods-this God will be a God for nature and humans together.

This God will not demand bloody human sacrifices for nature, nor will this God tell humanity to conquer nature. This God will tell nature and humanity to make harmony and live in peace-there will be no more massive wars of global destruction where inconceivable amounts of human beings are tortured and killed, nor will there be altars stained with bloody sacrifices.

This is the Third God.

So, God will change in the next century.

Actually, God is not changing. God, the Creator is still the same, only the human interpretation of God will change.

The Third God will influence and form the human soul and spirit in the coming three thousand years, like the first and second Gods did in the past.

Do we really need another God to answer to in the next millennium with all of our conflicts and troubles? Some people think we do not need more gods to dictate how we should live, and they believe that humankind can live in a godless age.

Agnosticism and atheism began because the belief in gods did not meet the needs of a new age based on intense technological development, scientific progress, and the theory of evolution. Darwin's theory of evolution completely contradicted the religious beliefs of nineteenth-century Europe, and his theory of natural selection and of adaptation based on scientific fact challenged the monotheistic belief in an omnipotent Creator of the universe.

As science developed, society has become increasingly secular. Even before the industrial revolution, science had challenged the Church's dominion over the secular world. The Protestant Reformation already challenged the universality of the Catholic Church and challenged the authority of the priests when they interpreted the Bible-the people should be able to interpret the Bible however and whenever they want. As society became more secular and industrialized, thinkers such as Nietzsche, Marx, and Jean Paul Sartre adopted an existentialist perspective on the universe that denied the existence of God.

Nietzsche said, "God is dead."

Karl Marx exclaimed, "I hate God!!"

Many scientists asserted, "Belief in God is superstitious."

The belief in God did not invent the automobile or make advances in modern medicine, and people, impressed with the inventions of modern science and with advances in technology in almost every discipline, wanted science rather than mysticism to improve their lives. Because scientific invention and technological advances demand the spirit of invention and creativity as well as logic and reason, people did not want to return to mystical solutions to their problems and wanted more knowledge rather than more faith.

We are living in an almost godless society in many respects.

At the end of the first kunmady, the era of the God of nature, the same phenomenon happened.

Many people challenged the belief in the nature gods at the end of the first kunmady.

Ancient Greek and early Roman society believed in nature gods, such as Jupiter and Apollo. Even though Greek gods and Roman gods have human characteristics, they are gods that represent nature. Poseidon is the god of the ocean. They had a god of heaven, Jupiter; Apollo is the god of the sun. The Greeks even had festive gods that celebrated drunkenness-Bacchus is the god of wine.

Thinkers towards the end of both Greek and Roman societies challenged these superstitious beliefs as unreasonable. Socrates even questioned the belief in the Greek gods that was common among ancient Greeks, and the Greeks executed him with poison for contaminating the minds of the Greek youth with atheism and because he failed to worship the nature gods properly.

One of his disciples, Aristotle, wrote about science and meta-physics, but he would never allow superstition to override his interest in science and logic.

Both Socrates' disciples, Plato and Aristotle, wrote from a philosophical and scientific viewpoint-not from the religious perspective of belief in the natural gods that was prevalent during their times.

Then, after people had begun to deny the old nature gods, a new human God appeared and everywhere in Europe, everyone started to believe in the dominant religion of the second kunmady: Christianity. Those people who denied the God of nature started to believe in the God of man, especially since they viewed everything that human beings invented reflected the superiority of human beings over the rest of nature. The God of man appealed to them because it placed man first in all of nature; they did not have to sac-rifice to the nature gods anymore.

The same phenomenon happened in Asia.

The people of Asia believed in the nature God first. As agrarian society developed, they also, like the Europeans that questioned the belief in the natural gods, doubted the authority of nature gods.

Many thinkers and philosophers had atheistic and agnostic ideas that did not support belief in the nature gods and instructed others not to believe in the gods of nature. They also wrote contro-versial books that denied their existence, even though when they wrote these books they challenged age-old superstitions.

Then, the second God came—Taoism, Confucianism, and Buddhism. These are all second Gods that place man first above the terrifying nature gods that demanded sacrifices. Almost every per-son in Asia believed in at least one of these gods of man.

In the second kunmady, there were only two huge human soci-eties built by non-believers in God.

One is Genghis Khan's gigantic empire.

Mongolia's nomadic tribes also believed in Gods of nature, but Genghis Khan himself did not believe in God, and the God of man had not yet reached that remote region on earth.

He conquered most of Asia, many parts of Europe, and built a giant empire, but the empire lasted only one hundred years and finally collapsed.

The next one is communist society. Communist society was built by the atheists who denied the existence of God as an illogical absur-dity; communist society states belief in religion is allowed but is offi-cially atheist. In the peak time of communism, communists almost covered half the planet. It seemed like they would conquer the whole world, but, as everyone knows, communist society collapsed into shambles seventy years after it started.

These godless societies share one common feature-they ruth-lessly massacred millions of people and destroyed all culture built by people who believed in God. They did not leave any culture or civilization on earth.

No one can find any civilization built by Genghis Khan. No one has ever found Genghis Khan's tomb.

You cannot find any civilization built by communists; except for the bronze statues of Lenin and Stalin.

God is the most authentic basis of human society and is the standard of human behavior; without God, there cannot be a standard for human behavior. God is the energy that fuels the human spirit; God is the leader of the human soul in its aspirations to spirituality. God provides value for human society, and God is the hope for the next life of human beings.

God is an integral part of a human being, and any society or individual who does not have God will be like a handicapped individual and a sick society — the communists and Genghis Khan's empire are just two examples. Without valuing human life and having hope for the future, one cannot live a fully healthy human life, and the belief in God creates value and a purpose to life itself.

God's most important role is to create the original human being, and people worship God because they believe he created humankind.

In ancient times, people believed that man came down from the heavens to the earth. All legends of the primal creation of humankind emphasize that the original human beings came from heaven to the earth. In heaven, there is a sun, there is a moon, and there are many stars, and in theology, the sun, stars, and moon become important symbols, symbolizing the descent of celestial human beings from the heavens to the earth. Usually, the original human being who came from the sun became a chief, king, emperor, or pharaoh, and the person who came from the moon became a queen or an empress. The people who came from the stars became subjects of the ruling family; they were messengers of God and blessed by the angels in the heavens.

In China, the emperors for centuries have been called Tien-szu, "son of God." In Japan, the emperor is called Den-no, "emperor from heaven."

All the Egyptian pharaohs, and all the kings of the Maya and the Inca, claimed they were sons of the sun.

Even American Indians did the same — the tribal chief claimed he was descended from the sun.

So, all the people in the first kunmady worshipped the sun or heaven. They believed they were the descendants of the heavens. Sometimes, the leaders said they came down from the heavens in golden chariots or with gold and jewels to rule their people on earth.

The second God is different from the first God because the second God created the first man by molding the earth and breathing life into the human spirit.

He supposedly made women out of man's rib.

The second God created man in his own image, so people of the second kunmady resembled the second God of man and worshipped the second God. By bowing several times a day and singing hymns, the people of the second God worshipped and glorified the man God.

All the information and knowledge modern man acquired through scientific research and technological development contradict the beliefs of the second and first God, especially the belief that the original man came from heaven to the earth or was molded by the man God. From science, we learned that the original man started from the depths of the ocean as a tiny microorganism, and because of evolution, became a modern man. It took billions of years to evolve into a modern human being from the beginnings of life in the first ocean, but in the Bible God simply creates man as an act of divine will in one day.

Now, we discovered and know for a fact that the earth created man, so the earth is the real God.

The theory of evolution was created only one hundred years

ago, but the theory of evolution is only treated as a subject of scientific study in schools and universities. Religion may be a private affair for many individuals, but religion, even though it contradicts scientific evidence that proves otherwise, still attracts people who doubt science.

Even though the theory of evolution is true scientifically, people have taken a long time to believe in it-nobody wants to believe that they are the descendent of a monkey. So, the theory of evolution was only taught in classes at school as a scientific subject.

This paradigm will change in the next century.

Most people will believe in the idea that they are the children of the earth, and the earth is the mother of humankind. Everyone will call the earth Mother Earth or my earth. But, even though people know that the earth created humankind, they won't worship Mother Earth like the first kunmady people worshipped nature or the sun by making human sacrifices. Nor do they worship the earth like the second kunmady people worshipped the man God by bowing several times a day and singing hymns. Instead, they will take care of the earth very carefully, and just like a good son will take care of his mother, the good citizen of the next century will make the earth a clean and healthy place to live for future generations. They will know that belief in God and the destruction of the earth cannot go hand in hand.

Every God, even the first and second Gods, has its own commandments, which tells human beings what is right and what is wrong.

The nature God's commandment came through a priest, which we call the shaman. When one has to offer a sacrifice, how many days one must work for building an altar, how to stop droughts and bring rain, when one should practice rituals, and how to attack another tribe and capture human sacrifices-all of these instructions were determined through the shaman. If people did not follow the shaman's instructions, they would be punished for their disbelief.

All second Gods have commandments, which were written in Bibles and holy books. People had to live according to the teachings of the Bible; otherwise, they were punished just like people who failed to follow the shaman. Sometimes, there are special commandments, which form the most essential set of beliefs man has to believe in and practice in everyday life, such as the Ten Commandments.

Buddhism has more commandments than ten. Some sections of Buddhism have more than one hundred commandments.

Islam has very strict commandments, such as: believers cannot eat pork. They have to bow five times everyday; if they do not bow and pray, Allah will judge them after them die, and they could rot in hell eternally. Believers must starve for a certain period in daytime during Ramadan and must visit the Mecca at least once in their life.

The Third God, the God of earth, doesn't talk.. There will not be any priests or shamans or angels or the tablets that Moses received from God. There is also no Bible for the Third God. People will have a difficult time to find out the will of the Third God. Still, we have to find out what the Third God desires because if we don't follow God's will, we might be punished or die. If the earth is capable of producing a man, the earth must be capable of destroying man as well. We must figure out the natural laws of the earth and abide by them in the next century for the purposes of survival.

We must follow the will of the Earth God in order to survive.

We have to find the will of the Earth God through scientific research, information, and through our instinct.

* * * * * *

God is an interpretation of the will of the Creator, and the interpretation of God depends on time and place.

Because the world is so huge, it's very hard to grasp totally, and what a person perceives depends on their limited information, knowledge, and vision.

Almost everyone knows the famous fable in which three blind men touched the huge elephant to figured out what the elephant looked like.

The first blind man who touched the torso of the elephant said, "Hey, the elephant is like a wall-flat."

The second blind man who held the leg of the elephant said, "An elephant is just like a pillar."

Then, the third blind man, who held the nose of the elephant, denied what the other blind men said and claimed, "The elephant is like a huge snake."

They couldn't agree together with each other, and, of course, they could never figure out the total picture of the elephant.

The conception of God changes according to the evolutionary level of man depending on time and region.

Some species live under the deep ocean, and they only have antennae to perceive signals from their environment through touch only. More developed species have eyes to see. If a species is more evolved, it is capable of hearing.

The ancient people who were less involved than modern civilizations believed in a tangible nature God. The tree god, the rock god, mountain god, and the water god were all tangible gods that could be touched and felt in nature.

Like the less evolved species, these people believed only what they could touch. All of the nature gods are tangible gods, and eventually, the nature gods developed into sun and star Gods that everyone could see.

The second God of man was conceived by hearing. Christ heard God tell him, "You are my son. I will send you to the human world to save souls."

Mohammed heard the angel Gabriel tell him the message of the God.

The people in the second kunmady were more evolved than in the first kunmady. Without touching, or without seeing, they conceived of the existence of God and believed in the existence of God — just by listening, they could discover God.

Not everyone evolved, and some people couldn't believe until they could see God. For this reason, people made statues of God — that is why the statues of the Buddha and statues of Virgin Mary were created. By seeing God, people who doubted the existence of God could believe in God more. They could feel comfortable and be assured that God existed.

Even now, TV shows are showing people rushing to see the figure of God. Sometimes, people go near buildings, where on glass, because of the reflection of the sun, there appeared Christ the figure. They are absolutely fascinated by the reflection of the sun and feel that Christ has come down to the earth to provide them with salvation from their suffering and the grave sins of humanity.

Sometimes, thousands of people crowded in buildings with marble floors find spots that look like the Virgin Mary. Some religious people bow and worship a figure, and even some put money on the figure on TV shows. Even in the era of the second God, tangible objects often symbolize God, and people sometimes feel these objects possess mystical auras inspired by God.

Sometimes, people come to see the Buddha's statues' tears or sweat. They interpret that the world looks so bad because the Buddha statue is crying. Because the world is so hard to live in and their lives are filled with impermanence, ignorance, and infinite misery, the Buddha statue is sweating.

Basically, these people are less evolved in a certain degree because they couldn't believe in God by hearing and listening from preachers or through reading the Bible.

The people who can conceive of the existence of the Third God must be highly evolved because the Third God is conceived by not touching, by not seeing, by not hearing, by not reading, but by individual instinct and vast information.

While people work on cyberspace with the computer, they see the wonder of cyberworld. People will travel in vast space and perceive the functioning of the universe through space travel. You can also look through the microscope and study the minuscule world of bacteria.

Then, everyone will feel instinctively there must be *something*; a superpower or energy that something created, organized, systematized, designed, and programmed to make the universe and everything in it function precisely and correctly must exist.

So, the Third God is very different from the first God and the second Gods. We cannot figure out what he, she, or it looks like; some people do not even perceive the existence of the Third God at all. Therefore, the Third God is very elusive and can only be found through information about the earth and the universe, which is by definition endless.

Throughout human history, people who believed in a more evolved God, in other words, in a more evolved interpretation about God, had an advantage over others and have sometimes led the world. Sometimes, they sacrificed and conquered less evolved people, and they usually became the winners in society.

The mountain god believers won against the tree god believers. Mountain god believers were defeated by the sun god believers, and they were sacrificed to the sun god.

Many people did not adjust to the new paradigm and did not believe in the man God during the beginning of the second kunmady. All of the remaining nature God believers were conquered, enslaved, often killed, tortured, humiliated, discriminated against, and colonized by the believers in the God of man. All over the world, this happened — to Asians, American Indians, and Africans. The American Indians, all of whom were nature God believers, were almost completely wiped out by the Christian believers in the second God.

There are some people who switched from the first God to the second God when the paradigms changed, but not completely, and they preserved elements of the first God's religion in their belief systems. Judaism is a first man God religion — Jehovah is the first man God — but the Jewish people preserved the nature God practice of circumcision. The Jewish people preserved the notion of an ethnic God because Jehovah made a testament with the Jews as the chosen and promised people of God. All second Gods are panhuman Gods, but the Jewish religion does not worship a fully pan-human god. Any God for certain ethnic people belongs to the category of the first God and not the second God.

Judaism is not a first God and not a second God religion, but may be a one point and a half generation God. Eventually, Jewish people were conquered by the second God believers, the Muslims, and were forced to leave the promised land.

They left the promised land and suffered a great deal, and everyone knows one of the greatest tragedies of the century — the Holocaust — was committed by second God Christians in Germany.

Hinduism is similar to the Jewish God. The main Gods, Shiva, Brahma, and Kali, are human, but Hindus still treat cattle as sacred. Therefore, Hinduism is also a one and a half point generation God just like Judaism. Eventually, they were conquered as well by the strong second God believers — the English conquered and subjugated them.

The Greek gods were also a mixture of nature gods and the man God; they had human shapes, but represented elements in nature — the sun, the ocean, and the heavens. Eventually, the Ottoman Empire believers in a second God religion, Islam, conquered the Greeks, who did not fully believe in the second man God.

Even among the second God believers that competed with each other for the power to believe in the God of man, who wins and loses makes a big difference.

Asian religions, Taoism, Buddhism, and Confucianism, are also

28

second Gods — gods for human beings. But Asian gods were not entirely gods for man — they spared nature a little from the belief that human beings were destined to dominate the earth. Taoism is about 30 percent for nature, Buddhism is about 20 percent, and Confucianism is about 10 percent, even though these religions still intended to make harmony with nature. All three of these religions placed man first over the needs of the earth despite their belief in nature.

Then, there appeared Western people who believed in a Christian God, a 100 percent for man God. Christians state that man is the only child of God; nature exists to be conquered. Then, believers of Asian gods and Christian gods confronted each other, and the dominant, most powerful man God religion emerged victorious.

The second kunmady is the era of man; therefore, all Asian gods lost and the Christians defeated the Taoists, Buddhists, and Confucianists. Most of the Asians who believed in the weaker second Gods were conquered by the strongest second God, the Christians, and they were colonized, humiliated, and suffered.

Just like in an Indy 500 car race, when the car equipped with a 1000-horsepower engine competes with 800-horsepower cars and easily wins, the mightiest second God, the Christian God, overpowered all other second Gods like a fast-moving car outracing every other car.

In the present vertical paradigm society, the strongest man God wins, and the believers in the mightiest god of all the second Gods, the Christians, have defeated all weaker believers in second Gods. They stand no chance against the most powerful God; in the race for power and authority over people, trying to defeat the Christians is like trying to cross the desert without water — it is simply not possible.

Among the people who believe in the same God, how a believer interprets the Bible, how they practice their religious ceremonies, and other religious rites makes a difference.

Based on an evolutionary viewpoint, more open and more free, less aggressive, less mythical, and less authoritative sects have an advantage over other sects.

Modern Western civilization started from Venice in Italy when Venice became a prosperous center of European civilization and controlled the trade and business in the Mediterranean area and supported the Renaissance era.

Then, the center moved to the Iberian peninsula — to Portugal and Spain. From the Iberian peninsula, they began the era of great voyages and reached most parts of the world, and eventually became the strongest and richest nations on earth.

Then, there appeared a revolutionary religious leader in Germany — Martin Luther. He made a new progressive interpretation about the Christian Bible, and many people in Europe started to believe in his interpretation of God, which created later Protestantism.

Ever since, the center of Western civilization moved to the Netherlands and Great Britain, and eventually, the United States. All the people of these nations are Protestant believers. After Martin Luther, the Catholic nations were no longer a leading force in European society.

In another major sect of Christians, Greek Orthodox, the cathedral is very high, the ceremonies are gaudy, the priest's hat is about three feet high, and the priest's flowing robes are golden and glittering. They will never be a leading force in Christian society and a center of Christian civilization. Even now, the people suffering and having all of the troubles from war and massacres in Eastern Europe are mostly Greek Orthodox believers.

People who need to have religious ceremonies with visual fantasy and audible fuss are less civilized, less evolved people compared with those people who can believe in God without sight and sound, like most American Protestants. Compared with the celebratory and festive Indian ceremony with drumming, the American Protestant ceremony is far less festive and is more solemn and quiet.

Religious ceremonies show differences in degrees of evolution.

Those people who preserve part of the first God's element in their religion and practice old religious ceremonies, claim religion is part of their identity, tradition, and culture, which they must preserve for the future. Identity, tradition, and culture are very important parts of human society, but adjusting to the new paradigm and following the constant change of evolution are more crucial for human society than anything else in humankind. If one doesn't adapt, one will drop behind, suffer, and eventually lose everything.

* * * * * *

Survival itself in nature's age was often harsh, painful, and short-lived. Even if death or enslavement by a neighboring tribe was avoided, it only meant the chances rose of contracting any one of a number of then untreatable diseases. Even everyday parts of life, such as childbirth, were often fatal — women often slowly hemorrhaged to death or died in the agony of a breach birth. The first God was a god of strength and might rather than of compassion, so believers passed from this life without any sort of spiritual comfort or peace.

After thousands of years of servitude to the emotionally indifferent gods of nature, humankind emotionally and spiritually needed a God who loved them. They needed to feel they mattered, and they needed a savior. There had been too many violent sacrifices on blood-drenched altars.

In other words, they needed a new interpretation of God's will.

The man-above-all paradigm was essential to the success of the second God because that ideology fit with humankind's emotional and intellectual evolution of the time, which is why the cornerstone of the message spread by the great second prophets-Buddha, Christ, and Mohammed — was that God loved the people.

The very character and identity of the second God symbolized universal love. Buddha loved people so much that he renounced a royal throne and life of comfort and luxury, so he could devote himself to helping others find enlightenment.

Christ's love of man was so passionate that he allowed himself to be crucified on a cross in order to save the souls of men.

Mohammed loved his people so intensely that he risked his life many times in battle and willingly suffered deprivation in the desert to come in contact with God.

Everyone was supposed to be loved equally regardless of heritage, culture, or ethnicity, regardless of whether one was rich or poor, healthy or sick, or strong or weak. Ideally, civilizations that believed in the second God would base their societies on their God's character and embrace all men with a selfless and altruistic love. Instead this ideal fell victim to a reality of man's human character — it is impossible to love everybody equally because people will always love their own people more.

It is only human to love one's own children more than the children of a stranger. It is only natural to love one's village more than one loves a village on the other side of the mountain one has never seen. It is inevitable one will love their own country more than another country, even though the consequences of nationalism and patriotism have often led to the destruction of other nations and hatred of strangers.

So, the original breadth of the love-all mandate was transformed and narrowed to a love-thy-neighbor sensibility. Instead of loving all men, people intensely loved their own family, friends, village, and country with a fervor that excluded all others, and over time, loving thy neighbor as thine own self mutated into a protective and fearful intolerance towards anyone who might be seen as a threat to one's own people.

The irony of the second God is that too much love ends up causing hate. If one loves one's friends, family, or village or country with all one's heart and soul, then anything that becomes perceived as a threat will be despised. Anyone who is not of the same community and faith are seen as infidels, barbarians, pagans, savages, atheists, heathens, and heretics unworthy of love, which becomes the justification to conquer and slaughter them.

One of history's most recent and horrific examples of love gone mad is Hitler. The term Nazi means National Socialist — the National Socialists' primary concern was for the welfare of the *German people* and it was *out of love for one's fellow German that National Socialism developed*. Hitler proclaimed his love for his Protestant and Aryan heritage so much that anyone or any group who diluted its purity or threatened Germany's real people, was systematically sought out and destroyed. Not only did he torture and murder Jews by the millions, he also slaughtered Catholics, homosexuals, and other "undesirables" who did not fit in with the ideal of Aryan supremacy. Those who were not one with him were a threat to his beloved Germany.

When Hitler said *I love my people*, the majority of people in Germany believed him and rose up in support of him because they agreed that the Jews were not real Germans and posed a major threat to the Motherland. There was very little uproar when the SS agents removed Jewish families from their homes and businesses in order to kill at least 6 million Jews by Hitler's own command. For the love and purity of his people, he had cleansed them of any outside influences that would dilute their racial purity.

Moreover, Hitler also believed he was a good Christian, as the cross on the Nazi flag, the universal Christian symbol of love, shows. And the truth is, the second God's message of love created, encouraged, and perpetuated this kind of genocidal hatred and fascination with racial and national purity. It is a law of earth that if a person has light, there must be darkness somewhere. If there is beauty, there must be ugliness. If there are winners, there must be losers. If there is love, there must be hate.

But as long as belief in the second God, whose character and identity foster and encourage love, continues, we will continue to see Palestinians killing Jews in acts of terrorism and extremism. We will continue to see Jews killing Palestinians because each side loves their people so much that they hate the other side as an enemy undermining their beloved community.

Reporters describe in chilling detail stories of ethnic and religious conflicts characterized by mass graves; people are maimed and massacred with machetes. Children are butchered in front of their parents. The systematic rape of Muslim women in the former Yugoslavia as part of the government-condoned policy of ethnic cleansing is a post-Nazi genocide righteously carried out in the name of God.

People wonder: how in the name of God is all this killing, torturing, and national chauvinism possible? But as long as people continue to believe in the second God, the annihilation, holy wars and other outgrowths of "love" gone mad will continue to spill the blood of innocents. As long as belief in the second God continues, we will continue to see Palestinians and Jews, Catholics and Protestants, and other ethnic groups killing one another because each side loves their own people so much that they hate each other.

The only way to break this violent cycle of destruction and hate is to change the way we think of love, de-emphasize it, because harmony is not only about maintaining a balance with earth and our neighbors but with our emotions as well. We need to *harmonize* love and hate.

This act of harmonizing does not mean we must love all people — whether we like them or not is entirely missing the point of the Third God paradigm. Harmony has nothing to do with love or hate, it has nothing to do with patriotism, it has nothing to do with cultural pride, and it has nothing to do with ethnic superiority. All harmony has to do with is balance and putting the earth's interests above all else. Harmony with the earth cannot be achieved if we set out to destroy each other by developing weapons of mass destruction and preaching hatred and insensitivity.

People tend to cling to the idea that love is a uniquely human attribute, one that symbolizes the special connection between God and his children — despite scientific evidence to the contrary that shows many animals are capable of love and complex emotions towards each other, whether offspring or human masters. So, it makes no sense for people to brag and boast about their ability to love, to conduct wars in the name of love, to cling to the ideal that love of one's people is justification for continued brutality and hate towards others.

What man does have is the unique ability to harmonize — because as the most intelligent species on earth, God intended us to embrace a higher ideal than love. Not that we aren't supposed to love our friends, family, and people; that is a natural and human emotion. But love must be tempered by harmony because a society ruled by love will forever be a society engaged in conflict and ruled by hatred and suspicion of those who don't share the same culture, the same blood, or the same national identity. However, a society ruled by harmony will be a community of people living in peace with their emotions, their neighbors, and people of all nations, and will bring the world closer to fulfilling the promise of the Third God ideal of all humanity working together for the common good of all life on earth and for the earth as well. This society is certainly very different from societies that set out to conquer the earth and destroy its resources along with all of humanity in the process.

Almost everyone is frightened when they imagine what death is like because they don't know what life would be like after this one, or even if there is life after death at all. Some people even believe that there are people who have come back from death and experienced the afterlife. Most people do not believe in these experiences because there is no empirical evidence for such experiences. The next life is all the time God's world; actually, nobody knows what life after death could be. The most significant reason people believe in God is life after death.

Almost all gods from the first kunmady to the present have promoted the belief in paradise for believers who have followed the commandments of God — the belief in a resplendent life after death. Believers in the first God thought that after death a person's spirit would reside in nature and inhabit either a tree or bush or other natural objects. Early man was comforted to know their ancestors were nearby and believed their souls would return to human form on certain holy days and live again for that day.

Similarly, those who worshipped the sun accepted the idea that if a body was properly mummified, the dead would come alive again and return to their original physical state.

Because early man lacked the mental development to imagine an otherworldly existence, his vision of life after death was simply returning to the world he knew in an altered physical form.

But the second Gods introduced the idea of paradise, an ideal world that was attainable after the death of the physical body. This divine realm — variously called heaven or Eden — was free from pain and suffering and was usually depicted as being located somewhere above the earth beyond the sight of man.

Since the second Gods were the gods of man, paradise embodied elements that represented man's desires and ideals such as golden palaces, beautiful fields where honey flows like water and delicious fruits, and, most importantly, as a place where you would be reunited with departed friends and family members.

For Christians, heaven was awash in white and souls walked into eternal joy through pearly gates surrounded by angels. For Buddhists, heaven was made of gold and gems, but women were not allowed into paradise unless they were transformed into men.

In Islam's Eden, the Muslim version of paradise, sparkling clean water is running, and people are wearing gold bracelets and silk clothes. Many beautiful women are waiting for men.

The one catch was that paradise was only available to the true believers who followed the teachings and commandments of the particular god. Those who failed to comply would be doomed to a different eternity — a burning hell of never-ending pain and anguish. The fear of eternal damnation was a strong incentive to follow the straight and narrow path dictated by the gods.

But as science and technology have developed, and as the human intellect has evolved, more and more people have begun to question the existence of a tangible afterlife. Common sense fosters suspicion that bowing so many times in a day has nothing to do with a person's intrinsic morality, nor does trudging to a service to sing, clap, and pray in order to reflect the goodness of a soul.

It is a fantasy akin to the tale in *Arabian Nights* where whoever figures out the magic word will open the doors of a cave that leads to unimaginable riches, and is as unrealistic as telling a student that the only thing they need to do to gain entrance into a prestigious college is to learn the school fight song.

As more and more tenets of the second God are proven false, the promises of a heavenly afterlife will also lose credibility. In the world today, most people want desperately to believe in the hereafter. They cling to the hope that this physical existence, this consciousness, is not all there is to human life — they cling to the belief that our desire to believe in life after death isn't simply a human response to man's awareness of his mortality.

The fact is, just as men need water to survive physically, people need to believe in a god and the hope of some kind of immortality after this life in order to survive spiritually. The Third God also incorporates the idea of another existence, although with our still limited understanding of the universe, there is no way of knowing how to perceive it or even its dimensions. Perhaps those answers remain a mystery until after we die and assume a different essence. It is a fundamental law of physics that energy cannot be created or destroyed, so perhaps the answer to the next consciousness lies in that part of life energy that remains after the physical body dies.

But paradise for Third God believers won't be filled with earthly possessions that are symbolic of the second God's "conquer more" character. It will be filled with spiritual peace and will embody the best of man and nature.

Whatever paradise is, it seems clear that the life we live now is a precondition for life in the next realm of existence. Just as we emerge from the world of the mother's womb into this life, our passage to the next world plane of being is equally natural. If an infant is properly nurtured and cared for, they will grow into well-formed, healthy adults. Similarly, those who live healthy, balanced lives, and maintain compassion with their friends, family, and harmony with the earth, will pass to the next realm as healthy and pure as a newborn child.

But the man who pollutes and destroys nature, who exploits others, who is righteous and refuses to live in harmony with nature and other people, will emerge in the next realm stunted, sickly, and deformed, like the unborn child exposed to toxins, radiation or other poisons.

A man whose legacy on earth is one of greed, power, vanity, conceit, and who participated in the destruction of natural resources for his own personal and financial gain will be despised and scorned as serial killers are today and will pass to the next realm with a corrupt soul and a life energy perverted beyond repair by their selfish and destructive life.

In the next kunmady, most who follow the Third God will come to believe in a spiritual realm after death that can be attained by following the moral path exemplified by living in harmony with nature and all of humanity.

As human beings evolve, the dependency on God lessens while technology and science develop, and people become more self-sufficient and produce what they need. The first kunmady people spent much time and energy on God. People in hunting society prayed almost every moment in their lives, so they could succeed in what-ever they attempted to accomplish in their daily lives. They prayed in the morning with the rising sun, in the evening before they went to sleep, and before they would go hunting in order to capture as much game as possible. They even prayed for their arrows before they would try to hunt down animals. Of course, they prayed for the weather to change; when they wanted sunny days, they prayed for sunshine, and when they wanted rainy days, they prayed for rain. For everything they wanted and needed, they prayed to God and hoped he would answer their prayers.

People in the second kunmady were much more civilized and organized, and they prayed regularly and systematically in society. Unlike the believers in the nature gods who depended on the shaman's whims, the God of man revealed in writing how many times a believer would have to bow and pray. No believer in the sec-ond God needed to spend time looking for the village shaman in order to find instructions about how to pray to God. The Bible could be found almost everywhere, and believers in the second God could read and interpret the will of God at home by reading the Bible whenever they had free time from work. Because the believers of the second God could depend on the written word for instructions on spiritual matters, religion spread everywhere. One shaman couldn't give instructions to hundreds of people individually, but the print-ed words in the Bible could be spread more systematically.

In the future world of the Third God, there will be no shaman and no Bible. Still, people in the next millennium will look some-times to God for answers to difficult life-and-death questions and pray. Even though science and technology have developed a great deal, people still cannot conceive of many events in life and have no control over many forces in the universe. Like Newton said, the size of man's knowledge is like a speck of sand on a huge beach when compared with the knowledge contained in the whole universe. The world that human beings cannot conceive and control belongs to

God. No matter how intelligent you are, no matter how much you brag about not believing in God, and no matter how much knowledge you have about science, even if you have a brain larger than Einstein's and you don't believe in a superpower, if your ship capsizes in the middle of the ocean and you are clinging to one small piece of wood for a couple days and on the verge of death, you would pray. If one day, despite all of your knowledge, you are trapped in a five hundred feet deep, damp, and dark cave with blood-sucking bats without food and water for ten days and are suffocating and losing consciousness, you will start to ask for help from God for a way to get out of the cave and breathe fresh air again under the sun.

So, people in the future will ask for help from God. People will not pray at every occasion as in the past like the nature God believers. They will not pray regularly or systematically like the believers in the man God. They will pray to God for help after they do their best and still cannot achieve what they desire, and only then, they will turn to God and ask for help by praying.

* * * * * *

After the second kunmady started, people did not believe in the gods of nature, such as the tree, mountain, and sun gods because natural objects and animals no longer embodied God. They still did not lose their original identity — the sun still shines, mountains flourish, and trees grow, and they fulfill the major role of the planet.

Similarly, in the next century, many people will no longer believe in the man God, i.e. Buddha, Christ, and Mohammed, but they will not lose their great identity because people no longer worship them. They will be respected, honored, and glorified as the brave revolutionaries who changed the course of human history. Without them, people would still be making bloody human sacrifices to terrible nature gods. As the most beloved philanthropists who helped and saved many people from being besieged spiritually and physically and from being sacrificed against their will to the gods of nature, they will be respected. As great teachers of humankind, they taught people how to live fairly and morally in a very harsh and difficult world. As the sun, mountain, and tree have never disappeared from the earth, the great founders of the second God will never disappear in human hearts and memory as long as humankind lives on this earth.

In the first kunmady, in almost every village, in almost every community, there were first God priests who interpreted God's will. They had a tremendous influence and control in the first kunmady communities because of their high social status and their unique ability to interpret the will of the nature gods for the people who followed the nature gods' wishes in everything they did. Then, people did not believe in the nature gods anymore and switched to a man God. The shamans vanished from society, and the man God's priest took over their role. In the next millennium, many of the second God's priests will disappear from human society.

But the Third God will have no shamans who will interpret God's will and no priests who will preach the Bible. What will happen? Scientists and scholars who know the earth and the universe more than other people, or those scholars who know how human communities function, such as philosophers, economists, sociologists, and anthropologists — those people will take over part of the priests' role and teach people how to live in this world under the belief of the Third God.

After man's God appeared on earth for two thousand years, there are still people who believe in nature gods — in the deep jungle of the Amazon, in the lush rain forests in Africa, and in some rain forests in Southeast Asia. Their lifestyles are much more backwards and uncivilized than modern people, and some of them still use the bow and arrow and run around half naked chasing animals.

There will be many people who cannot adjust to the new paradigm change. Some people will still believe in the second Gods and still practice the man God's religious practices.

People during the second kunmady, the man God believers, massacred and slaughtered the nature God believers as heathens and pagans, and they often burned them alive or drowned them in rushing rivers. Many women and children were treated like animals and accused of witchcraft. They were drowned, enslaved, and labeled as devil worshippers. People would try to find out if the so-called devil worshippers were using black magic and spells to make people sick, and they would drown women and men accused of sorcery in order to see if their magic would keep them floating until they sunk deep underwater while choking to death. The Indians were called superstitious barbarians because they did not believe in the miracles of the Christian faith, and many Indians were tortured alive for their beliefs. No one believed Indians deserved to be treated as human beings because they did not believe in the second God. During the Salem witch trails, many people were accused of witchcraft and hung. Many cruel acts like this were justified for the believers in the second God when they found people who did not adapt to their beliefs.

The Third God believers will not, on the other hand, mistreat, enslave, and abuse the believers in the second God. They are intelligent and knowledgeable enough to know that the first God and second Gods are steps in human evolution. Humankind must have experienced these stages in the process of evolution. They know in some parts of the earth that spring comes faster, and in some parts, spring comes later. So, human intelligence does not evolve at the same time everywhere in the world.

In the future, the first and second God believers will be called *mishiners* by Third God believers, which means "people who believe in the wrong interpretation about God." Unlike heathens and pagans under the second God era, mishiners will be treated

God

fairly in society and will be educated well so they can adjust to the new paradigm. They will be able to enjoy fully their freedom of religion, and they can practice old religious practices, but still they have to live in the paradigm of harmony. They cannot say "my God told me I can have as much as I want, so I will have one dozen children" or "our God wants a new church or temple, so a whole forest must be cut down and bulldoze the forest for the new church to be built."

Having one dozen children doesn't make harmony with other people. Bulldozing forests does not make harmony with nature. Even now, people of the United States have freedom of religion. People cannot have a religion that has human sacrifices because it is against the second kunmady paradigm: "man is the most important."

Christmas, Easter, Buddha's birthday, Ramadan, and all of the holidays of the second God will be preserved as a human tradition and as the culture of each ethnic group. We will have holidays for the whole world that will be celebrated because the founders of the second Gods are great benefactors of all humankind, not for one ethnic and regional group.

Among the thousands of first Gods, the last winner is the sun god. The sun is the most powerful natural object in our world — without the sun most creatures on the planet would die out. The Mayan and the Incan people are all sun god believers; they built great civilizations. Some of them we can see thousands of years later and even now — such as the pyramids. Since they lived in the point paradigm, all of the civilizations they built are based on the point paradigm. There was one pyramid in one area, and another pyramid in another area, just like points on a map. No connections existed between each pyramid, and there were no small pyramids around there.

Among the Gods of man, the Christians became the final winner of the second kunmady. The Christian God is the strongest God of

43

man in the era of man during the era of man because it did not consider any other species; this God existed only for man. Americans
who are Christian and Protestant made the most involved interpretation about Christianity, and in the vertical paradigm, which is the
era of the conquerors, they conquered the best land on earth and
built the greatest vertical civilization, with skyscrapers like the
Empire State Building and the World Trade centers. America became
the final big winner of the second kunmady and gained control of
the entire world.

In the future, the Third God believers, who don't believe in sacrificing weaker people and who don't believe in conquering others,
and who believe in harmony between richer and poorer, strong and
weaker, will build a more free, more open, and more fair, and more
transparent society, which will be called an information society
based on a completely different society than previous societies —
Harmonism. Under Harmonism, they will start building new civilizations based on a horizontal paradigm. This horizontal paradigm
may be very difficult to imagine because it has never existed before
in the course of human history, but change and evolution are necessary and without change, the whole world will disappear. More people will be free to pursue their dreams when humankind will live in
balance and harmony with nature rather than conquering nature
and humanity itself.

DEMOCRACY

The most significant feature in any society is its political system.

People living in the future must depend on correct and reliable information about the world because the next kunmady will be an information era. Just as the people living in the first kunmady depended on hunting for subsistence, and just as people in the second kunmady depended on farming, people living during the information era will live by gathering precise and accurate information for a livelihood.

In hunting societies and agrarian societies, people also needed information in order to live well — hunters needed to know where to catch the best prey and farmers needed to know about the changing weather conditions and the local environment in order to make a productive harvest. If a hunter hunted with the wrong information about the environment, he might miss a couple of animals he could have caught with the proper information. Without the correct information about the weather and the land, farmers could not cultivate their crops and would not be able to survive. People living in the next century will also have to possess the most reliable and valid information in order to survive; people who do not seek the proper information will be like the farmer that fails to learn how to farm well and cannot make a living. The sphere of human activity in the next century will be immeasurably larger than in hunting or agrarian societies.

Any mistake, however small, made by someone who does not have the right information could easily have a considerable impact on the local, national, and even global level during the information era.

No matter how strong or intelligent an individual is, no matter how skilled and how diversified a person's skills are, if that person does not live in a society with a well-developed political system, there is no way he or she can truly enjoy life. Everyone knows how people suffered injustices under the communist political system. Everyone also knows how present political systems around the world encourage and support material, cultural, and educational inequalities and that people would be much happier if an improved political system could be created based on harmony between human beings and the rest of the natural world.

After communism collapsed throughout the world, nearly every nation on earth began to work for the development of democracy. Everyone has hailed democracy as the most efficient, reliable, and most productive system possible in the world - democracy is unquestionably the world's best political system. But even democracy in a free market economy based on exploitation of human beings by human beings and reckless exploitation of the earth's finite resources cannot resolve our present problems. In fact, belief in free market democracy often creates and reproduces existing inequalities.

Now, society is experiencing a rapid and sweeping change from the industrial age to the information age, and people will have to find out for themselves whether democracy will still be the most effective and flexible system for the future information era. If democracy is based on correct information concerning the needs of people in the information age, democracy will still have to be updated and respond positively to the changes in society.

Democracy is government for the people, of the people, and by the people.

Simply put, democracy is only a political system for the rights of man. Democracy is the political system based on the belief of Christianity that man is the only child of God.

Maybe for the Christian God, the strongest God of man, it is true that man is the only son of God.

Now, we have learned that man is not created by the second God who claims he made man after his own image with dirt. We learned that man is created by the earth and not by a second God who created him in his image. And, we found out that man is not the only son of earth — all of nature, including the birds, fish, insects, animals, plants, and trees, is created by the earth in the same way that man was created.

In this century, man discovered the most astonishing truth — man must live together with nature and depends on nature to survive. Who would doubt that we need clean air, clean water, and healthy organic food in order to survive in the next millennium?

At the end of the twentieth century, human beings have realized that nature is not just a product to be consumed or a resource to be conquered. Animals do not live only to be hunted by human beings, and forests were not put on earth to be knocked down and turned into lumber to build houses. Fish are not living in the oceans and the rivers only to be killed by man alone and consumed.

We found that nature has an essential role: to maintain the earth, the only home for man at this time. We also found that if we pollute and contaminate nature, nature will get sick, and people will get sick, too. If nature is destroyed and vanishes from the earth, then man will also be destroyed and vanish from the earth.

Now, we found that nature is the most critical partner for man and helps man live on this earth and enjoy a good life. If nature is an important and essential partner of man on earth, then, humankind has to treat the earth as a partner.

Just look at how we are treating our partner, nature, which may be man's brother and sister because we share the same mother, earth.

We are chopping down trees everywhere, and, soon, there may be no major forests left on the earth. The trees, if left standing, could help keep the air clean for future generations and help prevent global warming, but we are continuing to knock down trees with no thought for the future. Every day, hundreds of millions of cars pump exhaust fumes into the air and poison the air, and many animals are dying from contaminated air. But we haven't stopped poisoning the air. Thousands of species are becoming extinct every day. Rare birds are dying out, species of trees are disappearing forever, and many animals have already been completely wiped out. But we haven't stopped destroying the earth, the home for all of these animals and plants. The ocean is becoming polluted and filled with garbage and toxic waste coming from the cities, and often beaches are closed because of toxins in the water. Global warming is continuing at an unprecedented pace, and El Nino's disastrous weather has reminded everyone about the fragile balance between the artificial world of human civilization and the natural world that we depend on in order to survive. But we haven't stopped polluting the ocean and rivers.

In California, thousands of starving sea lions could be seen on TV by everyone, and we know for a fact the thousands of starving sea lions died horrible deaths because of global warming and pollution. There will be no land left for the animals to live on once we develop the entire earth. Why should we callously destroy the habitat of animals on the earth and what purpose will our own greed serve in the future? We will have lost the ability to learn from the other species that inhabit the planet if we continue at this pace. Ecologists and biologists often claim that understanding of other species in the natural world and the preservation of other species is important for the existing human species, since life is a rare and precious phenomenon in the universe.

Where will the animals, the fish, and the plants and trees go in the future? How will they survive if we try to destroy them all? Nature is being destroyed in every country and in every corner of the earth, in the air, the ocean, and on the land, and it is happening so fast we can't even imagine or record all of the destruction that has happened and is currently happening — it is inconceivable.

If this frenzied destruction of nature by man, who believes he is the only son of God and believes in democracy, government only for man, is continued in the future at an unbelievable rate, we can know that there will be no man and no nature left in the next century on this earth. The only way man as the most evolved species on earth will be able to survive on earth is through a dramatic change from government for man only to government for man and nature on earth.

We have to change before it is too late, and we will have a new political system named Harmonism, which means man and nature must live in harmony. There will be no destruction of the earth as in the past and no conquering nature if we choose to survive in the next century. The developers who value short-term profit for their own advantage over the continued survival of the human species will have to be stopped by more conscientious and educated people.

Many people think that government only for man does not have to change because man is superior to nature — man can protect and maintain nature on his own in the democratic system. But has our alleged superiority to nature prevented us from polluting the earth and destroying ourselves with weapons of mass destruction and from contaminating the earth with harmful radioactive substances?

Many people are working for the Environmental Protection Agency, and there are many nature and animal lovers in modern society. These people work very hard to protect nature from pollution, contamination, and destruction, but they alone cannot stop the terrible destruction of the earth that our present industrial civilization is causing.

The government wants to protect some animals and has made a list of endangered species that must be protected by law. Some areas become parks or national land that people cannot destroy in the name of development, but only a few parks and protected areas cannot stop the forces of modern economic development and materialism from polluting and ravaging the earth's finite resources. Even the Grand Canyon National Park is very polluted in spite of the efforts of naturalists and government officials who wish to preserve the beauty of the park from the pollution and smog that has drifted from Los Angeles and limited the visibility in the park. Pollution in the Third World affects the quality of life in the First World. We are beginning to realize that the world is a small ecosystem, and the destruction of the environment in one area can easily and often dramatically affect other parts of the world.

All of these government policies and these millions of people working hard never provided a solution for the protection of nature. The air is polluted every day more and more, and in some places, the smog is so thick that people can't even breathe. Water is more polluted every day, and fish are found dead on the surface of the water everywhere. Rain forests are shrinking every day like melting patches of snow in spring. With acid in the rain, with cancerous substances in the air, with bleak factories daily polluting the atmosphere, with our cars and our other technological devices, will we be able to stop the destruction of the environment and can we know what sort of damage our present actions will cause in the future? What types of harmful diseases will be spread across the world from pollution and radiation leaks?

Exploitation and inequality, both of which are based on ignorance, are nothing new in the course of human history. In the old political system named aristocracy, which is government only for the noble man, common people, especially peasants, had a harsh life.

In order to support the noble man, they had to pay high taxes, labor, and provide crops. As the society of nobles developed, the noble man asked for more and more, and the common man had to work harder and harder. The noble man became richer and richer, and the common man became poorer and poorer. The noble man became fatter and fatter, and the peasant became skinnier and skinnier. Then, some progressive people, mostly intelligent scholars, suggested to the government that the peasants were dying, and villages were almost destroyed because of the heavy taxes and hard labor. They claimed that it was the responsibility of the government to protect the peasants. The government declared that crop taxes would be decreased from 80 percent of all the harvest to 55 percent of the harvest. Some influential peasants who revolted because of the hard life received quasi-lordship from the government.

In order to maintain the political system of slavery in the United States before the Civil War, slave owners did almost the same thing with their slaves as the feudal lords did with their peasants. In order to maintain the slave system, they compromised with the abolitionists who wanted to free slaves. They wanted to stop slaves from deserting and were afraid of the slaves' revolt. In order to keep slaves, some people suggested to hit the slaves less and to give the slaves a little money, such as one dollar a month, along with one more holiday a year.

But, despite all those efforts, the peasants couldn't be protected and could not survive in society. The only way they could be free from execution by the cruel lords was by paying taxes on time. If they didn't pay taxes on time, they were executed without mercy.

The peasants were only protected when the political system changed from government for only nobles to government for the common man. The slaves could only be protected when the political system abolished slavery once and for all and freed the slaves from the cruel slave owners. As long as slavery gave the slave owners economic advantages, like the huge corporations that pay their workers low wages and force them into poverty, the slave owners would continue exploiting the weaker classes for wealth and luxuries.

So, under democracy, which is government only for the people, there is no way nature can be protected.

If we want to protect nature, the only way is by changing the political system from government only for man to government for man and nature.

There must be somebody who will speak out for nature in the political decision making system. Under Harmonism, a political decision making system, such as Congress, will not be representative only of man - there must also be representation of nature.

The oceans would be represented by marine biologists, oceanographers, and other scientists, but also by divers, swimmers, sailors, surfers, scuba divers, and many others who share a great love, concern, and knowledge of the oceans and want to maintain the oceans against pollution and other dangers.

Mountains and forests would be represented by bikers, hikers, rangers, climbers, geologists, botanists, poets, and other naturalists — people who really understand the character of the mountains and forests and want to preserve nature against unwarranted destruction.

Some congressmen might think that it is foolish to have nature lovers and other people represent animals and plants in Congress. But how can people interested in economic development and the accumulation of material possessions ever express a real concern for the environment? Only people who really care about the environment and who are not interested only in wealth and money at the expense of other species should be able to decide about how to harmonize the human economy with the natural environment.

Political discrimination is nothing new in the course of human history and has been around since the beginning of recorded history.

Usually, political discrimination is a means for maintaining power and privilege at the expense of others, and those in positions of power have almost without exception fought to maintain their standing by using whatever means and ploys necessary.

In feudal society, the nobles did not want to associate with peasants. The nobles treated them as stupid, inferior, and filthy human beings. On the other hand, the nobles needed and depended on the peasants for their own livelihood and luxuries.

In bourgeois society, the bourgeois class does not like the working class — workers are considered to be crude, uneducated, and ignorant people. Yet, the wealthy elite depends on the exploitation of the working class for their luxuries and power — without subjugating the poor and subjecting them to minimum wages and a poor quality of life, they could not maintain their power and authority.

Skin color has also been the basis for some of the worst discrimination. The elites of every nation and the most powerful nations on earth have used skin color as a reason for the domination of some races by other races.

Now, the people who are rulers of the earth under democracy discriminate against nature because natural species have different shapes and different ways of communicating than man.

Nevertheless, all natural species on earth play a crucial role in maintaining this earth and should not be discriminated against. We should protect other species on the planet, and the desire to care for other species is a sign of the evolution of human species into a more harmonious, less exploitative, and more intelligent species than in the past.

Nobody likes mosquitoes, but mosquitoes have a role to play in earth, too. Birds eat mosquitoes for nourishment, and birds feed mosquitoes to their hungry offspring. When the bird grows, they eat the grass and tree seeds, and fly to different parts of the world, which spreads the seeds across the globe. As a result, grasses and trees exist all over the world, even in the most remote areas of the earth.

Even earthworms, have their own role in nature because they make the soil fertile — they are slimy, but we need them for agriculture and for the quality of soil to be maintained. As long as natural species do their part for maintaining the earth, we, as Homo sapiens, the most intelligent species on earth, have to accept them as part of nature, as a member of the earth community with equal rights to survive and to be protected. If we destroy too many of the world's natural species, the balance necessary to support the ecosystem will be disturbed, and it will be very difficult for humankind to survive on earth.

Another significant change in the next century's political system will be the breakdown of existing borders. There are about two hundred nations on earth now, and each nation has borders and blocks free migration between countries. The natural world — animals, plants, fish, birds, mountains, oceans, and rivers- might have territories and natural boundaries, but borders are artificial. Borders are intended to keep intruders out and enclose people in a particular territory and are completely man-made. Borders give us the mistaken impression that what occurs in one country is separate from what happens in a different country; in reality, events in one country also take place in the same world as events in other countries. Borders are exclusive, not inclusive, so if all the species on earth are going to live in harmony with the needs and interests of man and nature represented equally, then we have to rethink our concept of borders.

Borders appeared with the first cultivation of land, and they are a necessary consequence of the development of agricultural society. The idea of cultivating and conquering first arose in agricultural society; therefore, borders began with the invention of the plow.

In an information society, which began with computers, there is no need for borders. If you are working in cyberspace, there are no borders at all — there are no limits to cyberspace and the endless sources of information in cyberspace. Even the ocean is bounded by the continents and the atmosphere is bounded by space, but cyberspace has no bounds.

Because of the development of modern technology, especially with the airplane, mass transportation systems, the telecommunication industry, and computer networks such as e-mail and the World Wide Web, borders have already started to disappear.

As long as there are borders and relationships between countries are limited by the existing international law of national sovereignty, we will not be able to solve the critical problems we are now facing: polluting and contaminating the air and water, destruction of the rain forests and nature, the development and proliferation of biological, chemical, and nuclear weapons of mass destruction, the population explosion, drug trafficking, illegal immigration, and international terrorism.

These problems persist in the world because the interest of each nation is pitted against all other nations or because, even though all nations will deny that they are the cause of these grave, life-threatening problems we now confront, each nation has given tacit consent to the development of these problems.

As technology and science for mass destruction are rapidly developing now in every country for the narrow interest of each particular nation, scientists say that it won't be long for the nations of the world to develop biochemicals with which some terrorist organization or some hostile nations can easily terminate half of the global population on earth. We must have a strong system that can prevent these potential crimes against humanity and nature before it is too late. If we do not act quickly, the natural world will be ruined forever, and we will die out as a species.

We have to create a new political system which will break down the old borders of the existing nations and control all the earth: *the Earth Union*. The Earth Union will take care of and protect all the people and the natural world on earth in the next century; without it, the delicate balance between humankind and nature will be disrupted, and human beings will perish.

You might think about the United Nations and naturally wonder what the difference between the two systems will be.

First, the United Nations is organized only for the interests of the people of the two hundred nations of the world. The Earth Union will be organized not only for man, but also for nature on earth. Without representing the interests of nature, the tremendous exploitation of the earth will continue at an unprecedented rate, and no one will be able to stop the destruction of the earth. The quality of life of even the materially privileged elites will be affected dramatically since even they will have to deal with the problems of global warming and pollution.

The members of the United Nations believe in different gods, different ideologies, and different systems. Some are Christians, some are Buddhists, some are Islamic, and others are communist atheists. However, representatives of the Earth Union believe in only one god, the Third God, and one ideology — *Earth First*. All of our different beliefs in different gods have been useful in the past, but in the future, when all of humanity will need to unite and cooperate in trying to save the earth and all the people on it, belief in Earth First will be essential. Already, across the entire planet, Earth Day is celebrated every year and some countries encourage their citizens to clean up their neighborhoods and communities during Earth Day.

The United Nations is composed of people who speak many different languages, but the Earth Union representatives will speak only one language in their effort to communicate with one another — most likely English, the common language for computing. The United Nations is supported by its members' donations, and some nations pay more while other nations pay less. Naturally, the countries that pay more have more influence. America pays the most, so the United States is the most powerful nation in the United Nations.

But the Earth Union will be financed by usage fees for the earth. Any individual, any corporation, and any nation that uses parts of the earth, such as water, air, and land, must pay to the Earth Union a usage fee. With that money, the Earth Union will be able to maintain the earth clean and protect the natural communities on the earth while working to reduce pollution problems, educate humanity, eliminate poverty, and resolve other problems. However, the Earth Union will not control everything on earth — other countries will still be free to govern their people and resolve local matters on their own.

If the Earth Union does not work to resolve all of the most important problems and impose restrictions on nations whose national policy undermines harmony on earth, then there will be only more environmental destruction and perhaps the annihilation of every species on the planet. On the other hand, if the Earth Union controlled everything, there would really be no freedom at all for independent countries to manage their own internal affairs as they wish.

The United Nations is a good start for the next century, but this organization will never function successfully in promoting prosperity and peace for humankind. Rather, the Earth Union is like the expansion of the United States — the United States could succeed because people believed in one God, Christianity, and one ideal, human rights and human freedom, as well as one language, English. Now, it is time for the Earth Union to develop and create a more harmonious and healthy world for the people on the planet.

* * * * * *

If borders break down, maybe some people will worry that all of the people in poor nations will move to the rich nations and undermine the prosperity of the citizens living in rich nations. That's the wrong idea — everything will work in the opposite way. Now, every year, millions of people from poor countries illegally cross over the border and enter the rich countries in order to get a better job. The main reason is that the governments of poor nations tacitly permit those people to cross over the border and leave to the rich countries, after which they send them back to their home country. In the next century, anything that crosses over the border between nations will be controlled by Earth Union law. Any national government that does not control illegal immigration inside its border will be tried as a violator of Earth Union. If one illegal alien is found in the United States, he will be sent back to where he came from, and the government that did not stop the illegal alien from crossing the border will be blamed.

In the existing system, poor countries open their borders, and only rich countries try to keep their borders closed. This system will never work out for either the rich or poor nations.

After Harmonism prevails all over the world, the gap between rich and poor nations will be significantly narrowed. So, there will not be many illegal aliens nor problems with illegal immigration like during the present period. People will not want to leave their hometown to enter another country because, in their country, they will be able to make a modest and honest living if they work hard. The people of the various nations on earth will make a decision to eradicate poverty from the world and make a commitment to improving the quality of life across the planet.

Maybe some leaders of different nations who are despots, tyrants, dictators, sleazy and corrupt politicians will be against the formation of the Earth Union because they want to keep their country free from outside influence. In the name of sovereignty, these leaders will want to control their nation and their people for their own selfish ends, but if these countries will want to adapt to the new world, they will have no choice about becoming part of the Earth Union. We must evolve and change with the future whether some nations like it or not, and the Earth Union will materialize in the next century.

Expansion is the law of the universe — the universe cannot stop expanding. Human communities must also keep expanding and developing for the future; humans developed from cave dwellers, to village dwellers, to county dwellers, state dwellers, nation dwellers, and in the next century, they will become earth dwellers.

Now, Americans, the strongest people on earth, control the world, but in the next century, Earthans will manage the world. Earthans will be members of the Earth Union and will believe that the prosperity of all nations and peoples on the earth will need to be encouraged and promoted, and they will believe that all of the species on the planet will have an equal right to live on earth in a balanced and harmonious manner.

Recently, the world community wanted to find out whether Saddam Hussein of Iraq was developing dangerous biological and chemical weapons, with which, according to scientists' claims, Iraq could potentially massacre most people on earth. International inspectors were sent to Iraq to investigate Iraq's military arsenal to determine whether Iraq was developing and manufacturing chemical and nuclear weapons to engage in warfare with Western nations. Most of the investigators sent to Iraq were Americans because they possessed the technical knowledge to determine whether Iraq was making nuclear weapons.

Saddam Hussein, the president of Iraq, and the people of Iraq protested against the inspectors and refused to get inspected by them. They claimed that by the law of international sovereignty that Americans do not have a right to meddle with Iraqis' national affairs. The protesters had signs and banners that stated, "Yankee, Go Home!" and they cursed at the American inspectors. But, eventually, Iraq succumbed because of the American military presence in the gulf and the threat of nuclear warfare from the American government.

Iraq is a small and relatively powerless nation, but if larger and stronger nations confront the United Nations, there will be more difficulties ahead. If a giant country like China runs into a conflict with the United Nations, it won't be easy for the United Nations to make China comply with international law.

If in the next century, in any part of the globe, the same situation happens, people will protest against the American government, and the situation will be changed. American inspectors will say, "Yes, I am American, but I am American Earthan, too! I am a son of the earth, and I have a right to protect my Mother Earth."

No country can stop the Earthans from entering the country in order to protect the earth and its children, humankind and nature.

* * * * * *

Even after America became the only superpower in the world and influenced and controlled the world with America's mighty military power, there still are many small wars going on every day across the planet. Nature is constantly being destroyed, and people are being killed. Most of the wars are a result of ethnic strife and caused by border conflicts. In all of Africa, senseless killing because of border conflicts and ethnic strife is widespread — bloodshed of innocent children, women, and people can be found nearly everywhere. In Bosnia, the ethnic strife ended in a holocaust and genocide. The half-century animosity between Palestinians and Jews has resulted in many absurd and bloody deaths. The confrontations between India and Pakistan, China and Taiwan, and North Korea and South Korea over borders is unpredictable and could heat up at any moment and result in mass destruction and chaos.

The only way — this is absolutely the only solution that will bring a final answer to these deadly conflicts — is to break down man-made borders, live naturally, and create the Earth Union to establish harmony on earth for its citizens: Earthans. As long as people have a sense of national individualism and have strong patriotism for their own national sovereignty, there will be no peace on earth. One of the most important commitments, next to protecting the earth for younger generations, is to educate narrow-minded and locust-visioned nationalistic patriots in order to make them have an open heart and make them citizens of an egalitarian world community. We need to understand that we all want to survive on this earth in the future, and we would all like to see our children living in a world where diversity is accepted and nature is respected. No one will enjoy seeing other people or animals suffer unnecessarily because they will feel a responsibility for all the living beings on earth.

The next century will be an era of Earthans.

There will be many Earthans — American Earthans, Mexican Earthans, Japanese Earthans, Chinese Earthans, German Earthans, and African Earthans. Countries that are presently in bitter conflict with one another will put aside their conflict in order to protect the earth. Earthans will work together for one ideology, with one goal, and for one unique dream: to protect our Mother Earth and live in harmony with the diverse people of the world and with all of nature.

ECONOMY

Now, every nation on the earth is imitating the mightiest and richest nation that is the winner of the second kunmady: the United States. The American economic system is basically a capitalist economy, or in better words, a free economy based on money and class. Under capitalism, the wealthy have an advantage as far as material resources and education are concerned, and people are in competition for more money, education, and power. In order for the wealthy and educated elite to remain in power, they have to dominate the poor and the uneducated and make them serve their interests. Capitalism must constantly expand and grow, and new land and more resources are necessary for capitalism to spread across the earth. The earth is therefore often ruthlessly exploited under capitalism, and animals and other natural species, who cannot own property or represent themselves, are often exploited without any concern for their natural right to live.

The free market economy is based on two basic principles: 1) man is above everything in nature as the only child of God, or in other words, all of nature exists as a material resource for man's convenience, consumption, and welfare, and 2) the resources of the world are so endless that people can cultivate, consume, and develop as much as they want. Both of these basic principles, essential to capitalism, will be questioned in the next century and the coming millennium. We have already discovered that we cannot assume that the resources of the earth are unlimited.

We have now found stunning new information that human beings are not above nature and that human beings are not the only children of God. We have discovered that nature is also a child of the God of earth and deserves equal rights as man and that we must do whatever we can in the future to preserve the natural world and the species on it.

We found that this world is not endless and is very limited, even though we continue to develop the earth without taking responsibility for the consequences of our actions. Most people have seen pictures of the earth taken from a spaceship, and in space the earth appears remarkably small in comparison to the size of the sun or the solar system — about the size of a soccer ball. Yet, as far as we know now, only the earth in our solar system supports intelligent life and possesses a rich diversity of life forms unknown on other planets.

We found that, based on this new knowledge we have acquired, the free market system is founded on outdated and incorrect information. We must straighten out the free market economy along with this new information that we have about the earth in order to update our system. On earth, human beings and the rest of nature live together, but human beings and nature have a different character. Nature has a productive character, and when nature works, trees are growing, mountains are exuberant with pine trees and other life, and water is clear, sparkling, and clean. The air is fresh, and there are clear skies everywhere.

Man has a destructive character — when man works, the trees are cut down, forests are burned down, bulldozed, and cultivated, water becomes dirty, murky and brown, and the air become black, smoggy and sooty. Man is a species of civilization, and civilization is based on the conquest of nature.

These two different characters live in one world the earth.

Plurality is the law of the earth. Man and nature is like daytime and nighttime — they are totally different from one another but they depend on one another. Daytime is always followed by nighttime, and nighttime is always followed by daytime. When we work during the day, we rest during the night. If daytime becomes longer, nighttime must become shorter.

In order to work during the daytime, if we extend daytime to twenty hours, then there will be only four hours in nighttime because the earth only has twenty-four-hour days. If man decided to extend daytime to twenty-three hours or totally eliminated night for our own convenience, maybe some people will think that it will be good for man. But, the point is, if daytime existed all the time, all the species would become extinct. If we use the world for our own convenience 100 percent and leave nothing for nature, then nature will die out completely, and man will disappear along with nature. If we decide to have daytime for twenty-two hours during the day, and nighttime for two hours, many species on the planet would perish, and man will become tired, weak, sick, and eventually die. Even if we use the world 90 percent, very little will be left for nature, and since the character of man is destructive, eventually everything in the world will disappear, and man will follow.

Some people and some leaders, especially economists, claim that humankind can continue economic development, and we can still protect nature and flourish. This is preposterous. It is like claiming that we can have twenty hours daytime for man's activity and still have twelve hours nighttime for rest in a twenty-four-hour day. These people are ignorant of the law of the earth, and they are also blinding themselves to the real destruction that is now happening on the earth from human exploitation of the world's natural resources.

In earth, if daytime gains one more hour, nighttime loses one hour. Humankind gains more; nature loses more. Humankind's economic development is nature's destruction. If humankind develops one inch, then nature loses one inch. This concept is very simple, but some of the most sophisticated and intelligent people who are in support of unbridled economic development have failed to think of the consequences of destroying and polluting the natural world for short-term economic gain.

On this planet, as everyone knows, humankind has gained too much of the earth, and nature is on the verge of disappearing. If the free market economic system, which is based on the belief and the philosophy of cultivate more, develop more, and manufacture more, continues into the next century, sometime next century, there will be no nature left in this world, and there will be no remaining human being, too.

If humankind wants to survive and have a prosperous life in the next century, we have to create a new economic system based on correct information on the natural functioning of the earth. We have to make a different economy that will strike a balance between the different children of the earth: nature and human beings.

Economic activity should never exceed nature's productivity. In other words, man should not destroy more than nature produces. In detail, man should not cut down trees faster than nature can grow trees. Man should not pollute the air so much that the air is no longer kept clean. Man should not contaminate water so much that it cannot be kept clear and sparkling in its natural state. Man should not produce so many people that the earth cannot sustain all of the people. The new economic system in the next century will be based on this principle and new system: the balanced economic system.

In the next century, the younger generations will believe they are the children of the earth, unlike the people who believe nowadays that they are the son of the man God and are skeptical about the theory of evolution.

Children are nourished by their mother, and they should never harm their mother who has given them the opportunity to live and has raised them. In the same way, people in the next century will respect the earth's natural resources and will never take too much from Mother Earth; as a result, people will enjoy a balanced relationship with the natural world.

In the next century, the free market system will vanish from the face of the earth, and a new and balanced economic system that is harmonious with nature will exist throughout the world.

Why must we create a new economic system instead of maintaining the free market system? Because there is no other possible way of surviving on earth for all of humankind in the next century unless the free market economy is changed. The balanced economy is one step higher than the free market economy in the course of human evolution. It is an evolutionary step away from widespread greed and the ugly sight of poverty in the human environment. The quality of life must improve everywhere for human beings and other species if we are to evolve in an intelligent manner in the future.

* * * * * *

In the balanced economy, money will disappear.

In the free market system of capitalism, money is the most important resource necessary for survival and for the enjoyment of life. From buying an early morning coffee to buying a newspaper, under capitalism, human beings need money in order to survive. In order to buy the most basic necessities for survival, such as a house, clothes, and food, money is essential. But, in an information society, information will replace money and using credit cards is the beginning of the disappearance of money.

Without money, with information, a person can get everything necessary for survival.

But the primary reason for the disappearance of money in an information society is that money is against the paradigm of Earth First.

Money is the primary enemy of the earth — because of money, people destroy the earth.

In hunting society, bows and arrows are the most important items for people to survive. Without bows and arrows, a person could not catch animals, make clothes from hides, and acquire food from meat. Almost every person in hunting society had the bow and arrow in their hands, like everybody nowadays needs money in their pocket to survive. Society changed from a hunting society to an agrarian society. People needed the plow, and the bow and arrow were not necessary for survival. More importantly, the bow and arrow is against the paradigm of agrarian society — man first and human rights. Bows and arrows hurt and kill man, the only child of God in the second kunmady.

When the paradigm changes, everything changes. Bow and arrow, guns and cannons, and other weapons which hurt man are strictly controlled by the authorities in the second kunmady. Now, in the United States, people have the right to possess firearms, but they can only do so while strictly monitored by authorities. Large weapons, like cannons, tanks, warplanes, and warships are controlled by the government only, and no civilian can use them. In the same way, small amounts of money an individual can possess, but large amounts of money will be monitored and controlled carefully by the authorities in order to prevent the destruction of the earth with money in the future.

But, like the large sums of money spent in the arms industry in order to protect the citizens of each nation, large amounts of money will be used to protect and clean the earth.

* * * * * *

Multinational corporations will disappear as we know them now.

They are the most powerful and influential organizations in

human society now. They create and manufacture merchandise for people, and they have done a great deal for the improvement of the living standard of humankind by spreading material resources around the globe and by supplying jobs for the common working-class man and woman. People have benefited from the products of multinational corporations, but, on the other hand, as capitalism has developed, human beings have been controlled by these corporations in many ways. Now, they have grown so powerful and so widespread all over the world, most people think corporations will influence and manipulate humanity forever. In other words, many people believe that corporations cannot stop growing more powerful and more dominant in the world — it is virtually impossible for them to wither.

The narrow belief that corporations will never collapse is a locust's vision of the world. When summer is around, everywhere is green - green mountains, grassy green fields, and even cities are green. It seems to the locust like this greenery everywhere will never die out because of the lushness and abundance of life in the summertime. Just one night of cold windy air, and the whole landscape changes, leaves fall off trees, grass begins to lose its color — everything changes. Green mountains covered with large green trees with billions of leaves completely change and the trees lose their leaves, leaving them barren and naked in the frigid air.

When the paradigm changes from a man first society to an Earth First society, all the giant multinational corporations will lose all of the money they have accumulated from profitable exploitation of the working class, like falling leaves from trees in autumn that disappear. In order to supply large amounts of merchandise for humankind, they have to destroy many parts of nature and the earth, and if they continue, there simply will be no resources left on earth to be developed and exploited. It was O.K. in the man first society, and the multinational corporations were even heroes and welcomed by society because they manufactured

69

necessary merchandise for people. In the next century, they will be treated as enemies of the people because they contaminate so much of the natural environment and pollute the earth, which eventually will kill and contaminate all people, perhaps even with incurable diseases such as cancer, AIDS, and even other unknown lethal disesases.

At the end of the first kunmady, the armed tribes were the most powerful group in human society. With arms, they successfully hunted animals, defeated enemy tribes, and defended their villages. At the beginning of agrarian society, the status of the militia changed from beneficial to malicious from the perspective of the people because they had killed some farming people, who were members of the most important species on the planet under the man first paradigm. There is no doubt that multinational corporations are very beneficial in a man first society and in a vertical capitalist system, but when the paradigm changes to Earth First and a horizontal Harmonism society, the strong and mighty multinational corporations who once were beneficial will become very malicious, and it may be hard for them to survive. Nothing can survive against the paradigm of great nature.

One day, there will emerge new corporations who do not destroy the earth and still manufacture and supply merchandise for human society. They will find different ways to provide resources to all of humanity equitably without disturbing the balance between human beings and nature. It is a law of the earth that every civilization must adapt and grow by responding to the problems it faces intelligently and humanely; otherwise, we will simply disappear off the face of the earth.

* * * * * *

Land ownership will even disappear. The concept of land ownership began with agrarian society, and in hunting society, people did not own land. They had a concept of territory — from this mountain to that mountain, this valley is ours, and over the ridge is the other tribe's territory. The main tool of hunting society, the arrow, does not require borders to be used.

The people who used the plow to cultivate the land claimed ownership of the land. If people cultivate land, they own the land. If they conquer more land, they own the land. If they develop, they own the property. But the computer, the main tool of the information age, cannot have borders or ownership because in cyberspace no one can claim ownership. Moreover, in the future, many businesses will do business in cyberspace, and they will not have to have big property or a large building in order to run a retail business in cyberspace. They will not need big land for enormous school buildings for education because education will mostly be done in cyberspace. Many businesses or services that require large buildings will move to cyberspace in the next century.

Human acquisitiveness and greed for property will decrease as a result of cyberspace. Moreover, even if you own some property, you cannot cut trees down on your property, kill animals on your property, and dig for minerals on your property without receiving strict regulation from the authorities.

The most significant conceptual change in human belief systems comes from the philosophy of Earth First. When people believe that the earth is their mother, it does not make sense to own part of the mother's body as private property. People can use the earth and get nutrition from the earth during the next century, but no one can own part of the earth. If anybody needs to use land for housing, or for building, or for a theater, or for a stadium for sports, they will rent the land from authorities. Authorities will consider whether the purpose of this usage of the earth will make harmony with nature and other people's needs. If the purpose of the housing or building project is to destroy the earth and hurts the natural species and the human beings in the surrounding environment, then the authorities

71

will not allow the project to continue. If the usage of the land does not destroy nature or disturb the harmonious balance with the local community, then no authority can stop people from using a part of their Mother Earth. Now, because of land ownership, some people cannot have a house because they do not own land. In the balanced economy, everybody can have a right to use land for their house or for other purposes in order to live because people are the children of earth, and children have a natural right to use Mother Earth. Now, there are many people who want to use land for a good purpose, such as a house or shelter or even a school, but they cannot do that because of the greed of the ruling classes who have exploited the working class and left many individuals homeless. Anyone who wants to use the earth for an altruistic purpose in the next century will have the right to use the earth. Not only man, but even animals will have a right to use the earth — all the children of the earth must use the earth wisely. The system of inheritance of money and property will disappear because both of these will not be of major concern in the next millennium.

Throughout human history, the system of heritage has changed. In royal dynasties, kings inherited the throne from their ancestors. In feudal society, people inherited fiefdoms. In aristocracy, they inherited lordship. In capitalism, they inherit property, money, and stocks, but in the next century, nobody will inherit a throne. In the next century, nobody will want to inherit property, money, or stocks. An owner of large property will be a tremendous burden for all of society that no one will wish to pay for. Money will be useless and will only be a piece of paper, and inheriting stocks will no longer be practiced. If someone inherits the stocks of a corporation, and later, it is discovered that the company destroys the earth, that company will have to compensate and restore nature and the earth with every last penny.

In the information age, only information will be inherited.

Major multinational corporations will eventually become

obsolete and vanish in the balanced economy of the next century. Why must they vanish, especially since they have so much power and authority in the vertical paradigm of society? Who cuts down more trees than multinational corporations for their own business interests? Only multinational corporations are cutting down the rain forests. Who contaminates the ocean and rivers other than the multinational corporations? When Exxon spills oil into the ocean, millions of species of fish die. Who bulldozes the land as much as multinational corporations? In the quest for profit, mulitinational corporations have unearthed minerals, such as gold, diamonds, and platinum, and even radioactive substances from the earth, such as plutonium, in places as diverse as Australia to the Unitied States. If their reckless exploitation of the earth continues at the same pace without being regulated by an Earth Union whose interests will promote the well being of all the species on the earth, then humankind will surely be headed for a gloomy future in the next millennium.

These businesses are valuable for man, so they support the ideology of the man first era. But, these corporations cannot continue the same practices in the next century because the next era in the coming century will be an *Earth First era*. Now, they are the heroes because we are living in the "man conquers nature" society, while in the next century, if they continue to destroy the environment as in the past, they will be the enemies of the Earth First paradigm. When the seasons change, everything changes — even businesses have to change when the weather changes. How could you have a lucrative ski business in the summertime when there is no snow? It is impossible. People must meet the needs of the season. When destroying the earth is no longer the right way to live in the next paradigm, no one will be out of their mind enough to want to continue destroying the earth. There is no way to survive by destroying the earth when everyone wants the Earth to be first and not man. Businesses will no longer want to destroy the earth and conquer the natural world, and they will want to protect the earth for all of humankind and nature in the long run — if some businesses don't change with the new Earth First paradigm, they will fall behind and lose business.

In the next century, everyone on earth must follow the law of the earth — even businesses: "If you make a mess of the earth, you have to clean up your mess!" Major corporations will have to clean up all the mess and garbage they have made on the earth in the previous century. Like the tobacco companies that must compensate people they hurt now in this century based on man's interests, in the next century, corporations will have to compensate the earth for their destruction of the environment. The massive cleanup of the earth will be done by the most accurate, precise, and detailed information collected by the most advanced information technology.

* * * * * *

Skyscrapers will be left vacant or demolished.

One-hundred-story buildings do not meet the needs of the new information age industry, just like Egyptian pyramids, Greek temples, and European castles are only for sightseeing or have become ghost buildings. These skyscrapers are symbols of a vertical society and a consequence of the age of conquest. Those buildings are for those who conquered nature and weaker people while staying at the top of the vertical society; therefore, they will become monuments of a past civilization under the future horizontal paradigm.

These buildings contradict the new paradigm of the society of Harmonism, which is based on a horizontal, not vertical, paradigm. When building skyscrapers, the architects in the man God era did not consider nature and lower and weaker people. When the paradigm changes, these building designs must change as well. There will be many new buildings with a very creative and unique design that is harmonious with nature and the common people.

All gorgeous estates and large buildings which stand on beaches and on mountainsides will disappear. Beautiful beaches and panoramic views from mountainsides are the masterpieces of the Third God: the Mother Earth. Every child of the earth, whether man or other natural species, birds, animals, and fish, have a God-given right to enjoy the beautiful beaches and the mountainsides.

The most beautiful places on the earth, such as the Caribbean sea, the Mediterranean Sea, the Colorado mountainsides, and the hills in the Alps are occupied and destroyed because of the huge estates and other structures built for those who have power and money. Princes, dictators, corrupt politicians, corporate executive officers who became rich as a result of the destruction of the earth, drug traffickers, organized criminals, generals, and even crooks and playboys, in short, all of the winners in the age of the conqueror who act like they are in the animal kingdom in order to win, occupy and monopolize this land as private property closed to the common people. In the next century, these masterpieces of earth will be cleaned and restored with nature and will be opened to all the children of the earth, man and natural species, in order for everyone and every living creature to enjoy the beauty.

If there is no money and no property in the balanced economy, what will happen to the jobs and the economy as a whole? Will there be any jobs left for people? If there is no money, no property, no skyscrapers and luxurious estates to build, then most people might think that many jobs will be lost, and eventually, a worldwide depression will occur. Especially, most economists will state that if we switch to a balanced economic system, then everybody loses a job, and the whole world collapses. So, according to them, we have to keep the free economic system regardless of the price and must build larger houses and taller buildings while conquering more nature, developing more land for property, and spending more money for a good economy.

In order to build a pyramid, there needs to be thousands of masons, carpenters, and construction workers, plus engineers and architects, along with goldsmiths. Many chemists need to work on mummies. In those days, economists for the pharaohs must have told people if they stop building more pyramids, everybody will lose jobs, will get hungry, and die from starvation. So, the economists might have advised the pharaohs to attack more villages in order to obtain more slaves to build the pyramids.

The construction of *châteaux* in France and the Versailles palace, with all of its magnificent interior decorations, must have required thousands and thousands of skilled technicians and artists, even millions of workers. Economists for King Louis might have told him that if they stopped building *châteaux* and expanding Paris, all those people would lose jobs. So, they might have said that more taxes were needed to collect more money from poor peasants and farmers.

The economists of Czar Nicholas of Russia advised the same thing: if they didn't keep the system of czarship, all of the Russian people would lose jobs and starve to death.

All of the Egyptian economic system collapsed in spite of the economists' predictions. The French aristocratic economic system also toppled after the French Revolution. The Russian czar's feudal economic system collapsed and was replaced by communism. But people in Egypt are still alive, the French people did not die from hunger or suffer as much as the French economists predicted, and the Russian people are still in Russia in spite of the czar's economists who predicted the impending doom of Russian civilization. Now, these people live much better than these economists predicted and enjoy a better quality of life than in the past.

Now, almost every person in society, even children in elementary school know that humankind has destroyed nature too much and has to stop this wild destruction of the earth for future generations, but almost all economists tell the people, "You must spend more money and consume more merchandise, develop more land and build larger houses, and build more and more higher skyscrapers in order to maintain and develop a better economy for humankind."

Economists are the most shortsighted professionals in human society. Some other scholars and professionals, such as philosophers, poets, artists, and scientists, have longsighted visions that extend into thousands of years. Some of their work, like Homer's poems and Greek philosophical books, the Chinese poetry of Lee-Bai, the scientists Archimedes and Pythagoras, as well as the philosophers Mencius, Confucius, and Lao Tse, lasted thousands of years and will maybe even last until the next kunmady. By contrast, there is no economist whose theory lasted more than one hundred years. Karl Marx's theory of communism and the creation of a classless society, who is hailed by all social economists as the greatest economist in the modern age, did not even last one hundred years. All nations inspired by his theory and who practiced his ideas collapsed within seventy years. Keynes, another famous economist, who most of the Western economists recognize as the founder of modern economy, created a theory that is now in shambles. No economist has the vision for the whole season of mankind — *the kunmady*. They do not even have the vision of the locust, which has at least a one-season mentality. They have a mosquito mentality, which has less than a one-week vision.

It is a tragedy for mankind that people believe in these mosquito-visioned people's words, and drag the ailing economic system until everything in society totally collapses in a period of turmoil, such as a revolution.

Before the economic system collapses, we must switch to a better economic system. If we wait until all of nature dies, there will be nothing left to preserve, including ourselves. Only a balanced economy will save the world from destruction. Because every time society evolves one step higher, people live more opulent lives than in previous systems. This is the law of the earth — evolution. Once again, we began from bacteria and are now nearly two hundred pounds. Every step in history, man's life improves and expands. From the absolute monarch and feudal economic system, the bourgeois economic system, and the communist economic system, we have evolved and now we have developed into the American free market economic system. Each economic system is an improvement on the previous economic system.

In the man first society, people can start any business they want as long as they don't sacrifice, kill, and hurt man. The Earth First society, on the other hand, allows man to do any business as long as he doesn't destroy, pollute, and contaminate the earth; harmony between human beings and nature cannot be violated.

In a balanced economic system with nature, there will be much more small and medium sized companies and naturally more jobs than in the free market economic system. In general, average people who do not destroy the earth much will have a wealthier economic life in the balanced economic system. Humankind must create a new kind of food, clothes, and a new kind of house, all of which will not destroy the earth much. We have to find new automobiles that do not make toxic emissions, and new ships that do not leak oil in the ocean, and new airplanes that do not pollute the air. There will be many new kinds of technology and scientific achievements to respond to the needs of the environment and for creating harmonious living between humanity and the rest of nature.

The most balanced economy will be done in cyberspace, and without destroying nature and the earth, we can have a far better society for the whole world.

FREEDOM

Freedom is the basic tenet of American society.

Americans have freedom of speech, freedom of religion, freedom of the press, freedom to protest, freedom to establish organizations, and even the freedom to possess firearms. Because of this freedom, symbolized by the Statue of Liberty, many people all over the world have come to the United States in order to have more freedom and enjoy life in a liberated society.

Most American citizens believe they have all the freedom they could ever desire, especially since citizens in other countries do not have as much freedom.

Before the collapse of the communist society in the Soviet Union, most of the citizens there felt the same way.

They had freedom to have a job, they had the freedom to rest during the weekend, and they had freedom for fishing and hunting. They also had the freedom to drink vodka with their friends. They had the freedom to put their children into school. In short, they believed they had every kind of freedom they needed in life, but after the Soviet Union collapsed, they found the free society of democracy.

They realized that America has much more liberty than they

ever had in the past. Many of them were surprised and even stunned by the free lifestyle of American citizens, and they realized they did not have enough freedom in socialist society. They discovered that their lives were strictly controlled by the Communist Party, and they could only discover how oppressed they had been by comparing their lives to the opulent lifestyle of American society.

Before they compared their society to American society, they had only compared their lives to the czarist society that existed in the past when the common Russian citizen had no freedom at all.

There is no doubt that America is the most free nation on earth. But that doesn't mean humankind cannot have a more free society than American democracy.

Even though American citizens enjoy freedom and privileges as in no other country, there are still some areas where people need freedom. People do not have freedom from pain and disease yet, and even the richest members of society eventually have to face the fact that they will die and leave the earth, perhaps even in pain.

People do not even have freedom from crime yet, and as people in America become more materialistic and acquisitive, there will certainly be more crime in the future. Most of all, American people do not have any freedom from money — everyone needs money to survive in America. American people are living under the control of money, like Russian people lived under the control of the Communist Party.

Because of money, we have to get up earlier and rush in the rat race on highways to get to the office. Because of money, many people must work overnight and cannot sleep during the night — the incessant need for money has even prevented them from enjoying the most basic human activity: sleep. Because of money, many people must separate with their beloved family and friends — even though anthropologists and sociologists have agreed that the family is the basic unit of society, in an economy based on the pursuit of money, many people must sacrifice an intimate relationship with their family members. Most families are under constant pressure and anxiety because of the need for money. Because of money, people have to travel sometimes weeks, months, and years, either out of town, outside the nation, and even on the other side of the globe thousands of miles away from family. Because of money, many people have to do something they hate — some artists must become sales representatives for products they do not believe in. Because of money, many people have to do something they should not do — like developers who completely bulldoze forests and pollute the planet with no concern for the future. Because of money, some people kill other people — many murders are caused by the desire for money. Because of money, some people kill their own parents, wives, husbands or even children.

Every area in America and every field in the United States is controlled by money — whether politics, sports, arts, movies, or media. There can be no type of political representation without money, and some politicians even receive millions in campaign contributions from the wealthy. In sports, many of the stars in football, basketball, and baseball are concerned with increasing the size of their salary and receive exorbitant amounts of money while the average working-class person receives an inconsequential salary and can barely survive on a daily basis. The arts cannot survive without donations from the rich and the powerful, and movies are made in order to make money. The media as well are controlled by the desire to make money and often do not give the whole story to the public because people working in the media receive their money from the wealthier classes in society.

Even government officials, newspaper reporters, and organizations that in theory support the public need money and a balanced budget to survive. The era of big government has ended and government spending has decreased while the budget is being balanced. There is no escape from the pressure of money; there is no way out in the American economic system.

In the next century, we must have freedom from money, so we can pursue a more harmonious relationship with family members, friends, and other people. The pressure from money has placed an enormous burden on the shoulders of each individual in American society and restricted the majority of people's freedom unnecessarily.

Harmonism and a balanced economy will bring to the American people some freedom, not perfect freedom, from money. Under this future society, even if a person has money, no one can have a twenty-bedroom house on a beach because their excessive greed would destroy the environment. Even if a person has money, they cannot have a fleet of cars because no one needs such a large amount of vehicles. Even if a person has more money than others, that person will never be respected or a hero of society, but treated as a destroyer or as an enemy of society. The value of money is much lessened in society as a whole under Harmonism because the extreme of excessive wealth will be eliminated from society. No one will have to struggle to make more money all the time because money will not be important — harmony and balance with the earth and other people will be more important than money. Although this type of change is extremely difficult to imagine in our present materialistic society, there will be a significant movement in the future for massive change because the gap between the rich and poor will widen until the vertical society as we know it now collapses from an unstable foundation.

Because of the development of new technology, the price of necessities such as new kinds of food, clothes, and houses will be much lower than now. The cost of education, which now takes a large portion of the family budget, will be decreased dramatically because of the new education system on computers. So, no one will have to work at a job they do not enjoy, and no one will have to kill their friend or their father for money under Harmonism.

The law of evolution pushes society to progress and develop, and society must become more opulent and more free in order to evolve harmoniously. Because of this law of earth, in the next century, people will live in harmony, which is one step more evolved than democracy, and will enjoy much more freedom and a richer life than now. Every time society changes, more people gain freedom, but a handful of people lose their opulent lifestyle, such as Louis XVI, Marie Antionette, Czar Nicholas, and the lackeys of the kings and pharaohs.

People who have excessive wealth will have to adapt to the new society based on Harmonism and will not be able to live such lavish lifestyles while other people suffer in poverty; a balanced and harmonious lifestyle will be the right of every citizen living under Harmonism.

Since people living under Harmonism will be free from the tyrannical grip of money, they will gain much more freedom to enjoy their life, either for hobbies, or for art, or for sports.

They will have much more time than in the past; they will not have to spend every moment of their life in the quest for money and power and will be able to spend time with their family and friends.

In the next century, there will be a tremendous amount of new creations - new kinds of sports, arts, hobbies, and professions.

At that time, American people will realize how terrible life is in democracy, which is controlled by money, like how Russian people realized how terrible communist society is, which was completely controlled by the Communist Party. They would never wish to return to the era of moneymaking when every moment of their life was spent in competition for more money and power instead of in the search for balance and harmony with Mother Earth. Because of the horizontal paradigm under Harmonism, no one will have to work hard and fight to make more money in order to be more rich, more powerful, and to have higher status than other people, and anyone who indulges in this type of behavior will be considered a threat to society.

EDUCATION

Education is the process of teaching and learning skills and techniques in order to survive in the natural world and enjoy a healthy and fulfilling life. The most evolved species on earth have a certain way of educating their offspring; many animals teach their offspring how to hunt and how to protect themselves in a harsh natural environment.

People in a hunting society have a basic education and must learn how to find an animal, how to make a bow and arrows, and how to hunt in the wilderness. Of course, in agrarian society, people must learn how to make crops and produce a good harvest. In industrial society, there is much more diversity than in previous societies, and naturally, there are many different professions and skills to learn.

In human society, a large proportion of education involves not only the acquisition of skills for survival, but also information about how to follow, practice, and live according to God's will in everyday life.

In the second kunmady, most institutions are for teaching and for learning God's words - Buddhist temples, Christian churches, mosques, and synagogues, all of these produced religious literature and served as places of instruction concerning God's will. These religions are over 2,000 years old and are no longer appropriate for the present age because their teachings contradict the basic principles of modern science. As the scientific spirit developed, the gap between scientific fact and religious teachings is becoming wider and wider. Some people, in order to rationalize their outdated religious teachings, have claimed that religion and science are different. From a religious perspective, creationism is right, even though the theory of evolution is correct from a scientific and rational perspective. Because of this conflict, naturally there appeared during the twentieth century a gap between religion and science that is extremely difficult to bridge. Because of the two different truths and standards, human beings are in complete confusion now, and people cannot decide for themselves which standard is correct.

Under the Third God, science is the exploration of God's creation, and there shouldn't be any contradiction between religion and science. The primitive ideas of religion — that man and woman were shaped by an omnipotent God and the belief in miracles — are no longer valid. Philosophers, artists, poets, and writers are exploring God's creation with the human imagination, so there is no contradiction between art and religion. Scientists are now discovering that life is extremely precious on this Mother Earth and that the balance on the earth between human beings and the rest of nature is very fragile, and they believe that preserving life and preserving the planet is their responsibility and the responsibility of all the children of the earth. Scientists now believe in protecting life because we have already started to develop belief in the Third God. In the Third God's world, scientists will become like preachers under the second God because they know God's will by analyzing and taking care of God's work — the entire universe — and philosophers, artists, and musicians will be able to interpret God's will through creativity and imagination.

* * * * * *

Like a computer, the human brain can only accept one truth, but some religious groups try to put in two truths into the minds of young children — a religious truth and a scientific truth. This practice is very dangerous and confuses children and gives them two standards instead of one. Religion should never be taught as a truth that replaces scientific fact and reasoning, but religion is acceptable as a tradition, culture, and ritual in educating children.

* * * * * *

Before the beginning of the industrial revolution, most schools taught theology to their students. But when the industrial revolution transformed agrarian society, new fields of study emerged, and new skills needed to be taught at universities and in school.

Fields of scientific study and technological development began at this time. Physicists studied the laws of the universe and developed the atomic bomb. Biologists studied different types of plants and animals and developed systematic classifications of the plants and animals in the world. Sociologists studied human behavior, and so on and so forth. None of these fields existed prior to the industrial revolution, and the industrial revolution and the spread of scientific and rationalistic bodies of knowledge across the world helped develop and shape the modern world.

Now, we are entering the information age, and the study of every subject in education must be based on correct and accurate information. Any skill and knowledge based on outdated or wrong information must be updated with new and more accurate information.

Most books, theories, values, and principles taught in schools are based on the vertical paradigm of society in a man first era.

Many of them are based on wrong or outdated information, and we must rewrite these books and those theories must be reevaluated according to the new information acquired in the information age.

The first change will be the concept of history from the second kunmady — that man can change and create history. Since the beginning of the second kunmady about 3,000 years ago, people began to develop confidence in their own skills and developed the inner conviction that man can do almost everything that he desires. In other words, humankind can change the whole world.

Marx said, "Human society changes by class struggle."

Members of the upper class have continually oppressed the lower classes, and members of the lower class who will not bear the oppression anymore will eventually revolt against their masters and defeat the upper class. Then, they would create a new society without the oppression of previous societies. Therefore, people's willpower, energy, and determination can create and change society, and human history will change according to this law.

This theory became the most common idea in modern society — people can change according to their own wishes and make their own destiny. It is a very revolutionary and modern idea since people before the modern age believed that they were at the hands of the merciless nature gods and could not have control over the frightening and mysterious forces of nature.

Marx's ideas about the development of human history are incorrect, and his belief system was created as the consequence of the vertical paradigm. This theory may be suitable in the vertical paradigm of the second kunmady, a man first society, but it cannot meet the needs of the third kunmady, which will be an Earth First era. This theory was created as a consequence of industrial society when, with the development of technology and science, man became arrogant enough to believe he could make everything he wanted and do anything he wished. Many people in the world who do not believe in communism and who do not believe in the theory

Education

of class struggle still believe in the "man can change society and history" paradigm.

Only the earth and the magnificent nature of the universe can change the paradigm and history with the five laws of the earth, especially the theory of evolution. Because of the natural cause of evolution, human society has changed, and history has changed. Evolutionary changes in human society are like the changing seasons in the natural world. If the natural season changes, man has to change, too.

If winter changes to spring, people must change their clothes, and no one would wear a thick overcoat in the spring in order to survive.

People can easily perceive the change of the seasons in nature, but people cannot easily see the changes in evolution of the human mind. Because of the natural cause of evolution, the human brain has evolved, and the human mind has changed. These evolutionary changes are natural causes completed by the law of the earth.

People cannot change the law of the earth — evolution.

Humanity can only adjust and follow the changes that occur in evolution in order to survive.

Some people might like cold weather because they enjoy skiing or skating. So, maybe they do not want the warm spring to come, but still, they must follow the change of the seasons, otherwise, they might drop behind or suffer. Maybe, sometime, they will not be able to survive.

Each different society in human history is a step in the natural course of evolution. People have only followed new changes in evolution from century to century, and people who did not follow the change are banished from society or suffered while dropping behind.

Like a man who only likes the wintertime and does not want to change to spring, a man who only likes aristocracy, wants to keep his lordship, and does not want to follow democracy, must have suffered or dropped behind in a democratic society.

A new form of education will begin in the next century and will completely change the erroneous notion that humankind can change everything. Human beings will have to follow the law of Mother Earth; otherwise, if we still believe that man can change history and work against the paradigm of earth, then people will perish or suffer unnecessary misery.

Most of the subjects in education that students are presently learning are based on how to conquer the earth. In any subject, whether politics, law, economics, history, and sociology, even science, conquering the earth, conquering weaker people, and conquering more markets — these ideas are taught. Because of the vertical system, schools teach students to reach the top of corporations, of society, of the class, and of course, the top of the world, and the people at the bottom of corporations even desire to one day improve their lives and become more powerful and attain a higher status.

In order to do so, more is always better — more money, more property, more market shares, more power, and more fame is taught to the people. This paradigm will change, and many subjects and curriculum must be changed from the idea of conquering the earth to harmonizing with the earth. Education will be centered on how to harmonize with nature, and how to harmonize with different kinds of people from different ethnicities, races, backgrounds, ages, with people who have different hobbies and different personalities. People must learn that more is not always better, higher is not always better, and sometimes, establishing balance and harmony is better.

No matter how much education a person possesses, no matter what technique that person knows, if they do not have the technical skill that meets the paradigm of society, then they have acquired unnecessary skills.

According to scientists, historians, and archaeologists, the construction of pyramids involved a great knowledge of geometry, mathematics, engineering, and of architecture. Even now, we have trouble imagining how the ancient Egyptians could build a construction as awesome as the pyramid without modern scientific technology. We do not know how they carved the huge stones with precision to make blocks for the pyramid and how each block was stacked precisely onto other blocks.

When we compare the pyramid to some of the most modern architectural wonders, the pyramid is a sign of an equally evolved and advanced society.

We still do not know how mummies were embalmed and have not developed the technology to embalm, but we do not need the technology to mummify the bodies of the deceased or pyramids to entomb the dead because we live under a different paradigm.

We have developed new technology in our present age that is entirely different from the technology the Egyptians used in order to adapt to a new paradigm.

Technology changes when the paradigm changes, and the skills and education necessary for survival change as well. These changes are the consequence of the natural law of earth: *evolution*. No matter how developed the technology of a civilization is, if it does not meet the needs of a new paradigm, it vanishes along with the old paradigm.

In the peak time of the Soviet Union in the 1960s, only 30 years ago, Moscow University was one of the most enviable educational institutions in the world. But, after socialism collapsed, most of the knowledge, skills, and education became useless. For example, the young people who learned about the socialist economy, which is a state-planned economic system, could not find a job with the theory that they struggled to learn in school. No nation on the earth would use the state planning economic system anymore. They received the highest degree for their own work, but they had trouble finding a place to use their knowledge.

The most prestigious institutes, where students are learning how to conquer and destroy the earth, might be useless in the next century when the paradigm shifts from conquering the earth to harmony with the earth..

If educational institutions do not modify the curriculum from the vertical paradigm with an uneven economy to the horizontal paradigm with a balanced economy, they must change if they want to be successful in the next century.

Once again, in the first kunmady, the people who sacrificed more human beings became the winner. In the second kunmady, the people who conquered more people and nature became winners. But, in the third kunmady, those who make harmony with people and nature will be winners and have the proper information to survive.

When seasons change, the landscape of nature changes.

When winter is over, and spring comes, the icy white snow that covers the land melts and colorful flowers begin to blossom everywhere. When the paradigm changes in human society, the landscape of human communities changes.

The landscape in the present vertical society — houses, buildings, schools, stadiums, churches, shopping centers, and industrial complexes are designed to meet the paradigm based on conquering. Some of them are very artistic and well designed, especially temples like the Taj Mahal in India, Buddhist temples, Islamic mosques, and the ruins of ancient Rome. But, otherwise, most buildings are bland, uninspiring, and monotonous. Many modern neighborhoods and even entire cities have houses that are exactly the same — absolutely nothing is unique about each house.

After capitalism prevailed on the earth, some buildings were designed for showing off wealth and are exceptionally high. Some buildings are so ugly and dull because the designers of the building wanted to economize. None of these buildings consider the value of nature, and also, there is no consideration for the common people in the design of these buildings. The bleak landscape in modern neighborhoods does not create a harmonious atmosphere for human beings and for nature as well. Often, one-hundred-story buildings stand next to collapsed shacks, just like in many modern cities where millionares live in the same area as the homeless.

In the next century, the younger generation will create new landscapes in every human society, and in order to do so, young architects, developers, artists, and reformers of society will get involved in the most important project on earth for the future: building a new civilization based on harmony with nature and all of humanity. Students from many different professions and backgrounds will cooperate in order to build this unprecedented civlization — a civilization inconceivable in previous centuries.

* * * * * *

Before the change in the natural landscapes during seasons change, the temperature of the air must be changed.

Before the change in the paradigm during the transition from the second kunmady to the third kunmady, energy will be changed.

Before humankind builds a new civilization, humankind must change the existing energy.

There are essentially two kinds of energy used in modern society: nuclear energy and oil.

Nuclear energy is safe in the short run, but nobody is sure that nuclear energy is not dangerous in the long run — we have already experienced many nuclear disasters, such as leakages in nuclear power plants. No matter how secure nuclear power plants are, they always produce deadly radioactive waste. There are few places where we can put nuclear waste without endangering the environment, and even now, we have a problem with storing nuclear waste. Because of the human need for convenience, we have generated very hazardous pollution and radioactive waste, which acts against the new paradigm based on harmony with nature.

Oil is a primary source of energy that pollutes the air with smog and soot from gas emissions, contaminates oceans with oil leaks, and destroys the earth through drilling thousands of feet down into the earth's surface.

Some people say, "Pumping oil and using oil is O.K. as long as we are cautious, and we refine oil safely." No matter how cautiously pumped, no matter where and how we refine oil, no matter how much we control emissions in the future, still, every day, all over the globe, oil keeps leaking in the ocean and poisonous gases are released into the atmosphere. Smog is worsening every day, and in some cities, the air is difficult to breathe.

Some people say, especially oil company representatives, "If humankind doesn't pump or use oil, then there will be no cars running on the road. When a man from New York wants to see his daughter in Los Angeles, he will have to walk across the continent. Everybody on earth will lose a job and will get hungry, die, and the world will collapse."

These people have sparrow brains and a snail's vision. If humankind stops pumping oil, soon humankind will find a better source of energy and will have an improved life. Humankind has the necessary capability, creativity, and intelligence to do so.

If pumping oil from the earth and using it is hazardous not only to man but to the rest of nature, it must be against the law of the earth. Furthermore, drilling thousands of feet down and pumping oil from the earth might be like sucking vital liquids from the earth. In the next century, the Earth First era, it will be very hard to justify drilling with gigantic metal drills into the depths of the body of Mother Earth, the mother of all humankind and all nature. The Mother Earth is also a living and evolving body, and without her resources, without fresh air, minerals, and water, as well as plants, forests, and evolving ecosystems, human existence would soon vanish.

In the next century, we have to find the energy source from outside earth in order to protect the earth. At this point, solar, wind, and tidal energy will be the only alternative energy sources in the next century. If we develop efficient technology to absorb and store all one sunny day's solar energy on earth, all humankind would live a much more civilized life for more than one hundred years, some scientists say. In the next century, developing such technology is the most important part of education.

In the next century, in order to protect animals and trees, mankind has to have an alternative food resource and another resource than trees for building houses. If people believe that animals have the same right to survive as humankind, then many people will be reluctant to butcher and kill animals for food. We must create food with enough nutrition that tastes like beef and pork without killing animals who have a natural right to exist on earth.

The main reason humankind has cut down trees is to acquire lumber for building houses and other buildings. Unless humankind can create an alternative tree, we cannot maintain the forests. In order to create tasty, alternative forms of food and alternative types of trees, humankind must develop genetic science. Humankind must create either alternative materials other than trees or another kind of tree that grows faster than human beings can consume. Or, instead of chopping down trees for a house, we should create a new kind of tree that grows and forms like a house, so people can live in the tree after the tree is fully grown in the form of a two or three story house. In this house, men and trees can live together in harmony; there will be no senseless destruction of trees. In the next century, under Harmonism, genetic engineering will be the major industry of society like deer hunting in hunting society, and corn or wheat in an agrarian society. The educational system will be reorganized from the existing system to meet the design of the new society.

There is another important reason that genetic science will be developed in the future and through the next three thousand years.

Genetic science will be the major industry of society and play a major role in the next three thousand years.

Humankind is now heading to space life, and we have already landed on the moon and sent satellites to Mars to investigate its surface. We will begin by exploring more and more space, and we will develop more advanced and sophisticated technology until we can make more frequent journeys in order to gather more information. We will eventually find the most suitable place for living, whether in this solar system or in a more distant solar system. We might enter into contact with alien life forms. Someday, we will move from the small crowded earth and will live in limitless space.

After the Greeks and Romans discovered navigation technology by watching stars and sailed around the Mediterranean Sea, it took more than two thousand years for Columbus to reach another continent. After that, it took more than five hundred years for man to reach to every corner of the earth with a boat. In order to reach everywhere in the world, with a sail, we could not accomplish travel fast enough and reach every place in the world, so we developed the motor.

If we want to reach many different planets and galaxies, the existing engine does not have the power to travel there. The rocket engine could not reach them because most stars are millions and even billions of miles away from the earth. The speed generated by rocket engines would not ever propel space shuttles that far.

In order to get prepared for space life in the future, which might occur in the fourth kunmady, in the next three thousand years, we must develop genetic science and engineering. The beginning of the next century is the beginning of the third kunmady. In order to protect nature and improve human life, genetic science will be a booming part of education. Of course, genetic engineering must meet the paradigm of the next century — the paradigm of Earth First and harmony with nature and man. Even science must live in the paradigm of the next century. Anyone who engages in science for destruction of the earth will be closely monitored and scrutinized by the Earth Union, and the misuse of science against the interests of the earth will be treated as a serious crime.

Genetic science will be the most important industry for the information age.

Many sciences and technical skills are mostly based on destroying the earth and nature. We have to switch from the destructive style of education to more productive education in the next century. Genetic engineering will be one of the more productive types of education.

There will be a big change in the educational system in the next century.

Courses in universities, elementary schools, and high schools will be taught through the Internet. English will be the primary language to use in cyberspace classrooms all over the world. From thousands of miles away, people will be able to take any class they desire from any country and any nation. Even people in the hillside of the Himalayas will be able to listen to the lectures of famous professors in Harvard simultaneously along with people in the United States. The cost of education will be dramatically less in the future, and the best quality education will be available at a very low price. Because working hours will be shorter in the next century, people will have more time to spend educating themselves.

Education essentially means the transmission of more information. If any person, or any people, or any nation want to be successful in the next century, they must spend much of their energy for education. Otherwise, they will fail, drop behind, or even vanish from the earth.

MORALS AND ETHICS

Among all of the species on the earth, the distinguishing feature of human beings is the capacity for ethics and morals. Human beings began to believe in ethics and morals after they developed the ability to believe in God. Since the first kunmady, God became the base and standard of morals and ethics in society. So, most religious people in society usually become the most ethical and moral people.

In hunting society, a hunter left his home in the early morning for hunting, and his daily life started with bowing three times to the god of the mountain or when he faced the sun and worshipped the god of the sun.

When he caught animals, he offered the best part of the animal to the god first as a sign of humility. He often attacked another tribe or village and caught other tribesmen and made human sacrifices as an offering for his god, and some captives were used as slaves that built the altars of the gods.

When it was necessary for the community to appease angry gods because of their wrath at the natural cause of hurricanes or droughts or earthquakes or spreading epidemics, or in order to defend villages from other attacking tribes, sometimes he offered to the god his own children. Most religious men would volunteer themselves to be sacrificed to placate the angry gods.

In farming societies, a good farmer begins everyday life by making a prayer before breakfast and works hard all day on the farm. In the evening, he has dinner with the whole family together and reads the Bible before he goes to bed. He attends church services every Sunday with the whole family and helps other people whenever they need assistance. He contributes one-tenth of whatever he harvests to God and donates that portion of the harvest to the church. He believes in the Ten Commandments and practices them in everyday life.

These people are the most religious and most ethical and moral people in agrarian society. In industrial society, a person who works hard to receive a quality education, attends a good school, studies diligently, graduates, finds a job or a business, works very hard at his job, and takes care of his family and treats his neighbor as his friend is ethical and moral. He attends church services every Sunday and is involved in community activities. He donates a portion of his earnings to charitable institutions, whether helping the homeless, alcoholics, etc. When he gets old, before he dies, most of his life savings are donated for philanthropic purposes.

Of course, he believes in the Ten Commandments and practices them in everyday life. This person is the typical ethical and moral person in industrial society.

As the end of the millenium approaches, ethics and morals are vanishing into thin air. The belief in the second God is disappearing and less people are attending church. Especially, the elite of society and the younger generation seldom attend church. Sometimes, they attend church, but not because of their belief - because of social custom and cultural practices. The elite (the prime movers of society) and the young generation (the future hope of society)are keeping away from church and shun the second God. Statistics say that less than 10 percent of people believe in the Ten Commandments compared to a century ago when over 90 percent believed in the Ten Commandments and attended church regularly. Naturally, ethical and moral standards are plummeting, and as a result society has become very superficial and corrupt.

Every day the news and TV show unimaginable crimes — murderers cruelly attacking their victims, robberies, rapists, abused children, alcoholism, and manipulative political scandals. For example, a disguised man enters into a convenience store with a gun and holds the cashier at gunpoint. The robber kills the cashier — only for a six-pack. Senseless crimes like this happen daily in cities in the modern world. But that's not the only example that can be given — imagine an innocent girl raped on a college campus by a group of men. In a place where the younger generation studies truth and prepares to contribute to society, a girl is raped and her dead body abandoned on the campus. Unsuspecting innocent people are often murdered for no reason at all. There are so many examples of crime in modern society that violence has become a commonplace occurence.

Aside from violent crimes, there are many white-collar crimes, such as cheating, corruption, extortion, and deception in almost every corner of society. It seems like the ethical and moral code is leaving the human heart.

Many people, especially religious leaders, are tormented by the complete collapse of ethics in modern society. The only way they believe we can revive the moral and ethical spirit is by returning to the belief in God and attending church.

But this is not the first time that moral and ethical corruption has occurred.

At the end of the first kunmady, almost exactly the same phenomenon happened. At the end of the first kunmady, people started to doubt the nature gods, and they did not want to believe in the shaman's interpretation of the nature gods. The younger generation did not want to attend rituals, build altars or drink human blood, just like people in the present time do not want to go to church and do not want to believe in the preacher's words. Instead, they chopped the holy trees of the tree god and built their own shelter. They burned down moutainsides where the mountain god was worshipped, and they cultivated wheat. The preachers and the village elders cried and felt tormented; they felt God would punish people for their ignorance and a big disaster would eventually come. The tree gods would not make any fruits on the trees, and the mountain god would not have any animals on it. The sun god would disappear, and the whole world would get dark and vanish. The only way to appease God again would be to bring good harvests and to hunt well while attending ceremonies, which would last sometimes three days and end with more human sacrifices.

But people never go back to the old God and old moral beliefs. People find a new God, new ethics, and new moral beliefs to meet the needs of their time.

When winter is nearly finished and spring is just about to arrive, during a transitional period between seasons, in the nighttime, it is very cold like in winter, and in the daytime, it is warm like spring. The snow is melting in the daytime and everything is very messy — that's where we are at in society. In a period of transition, there are two standards because the transitional season has the characteristics of winter and spring — just like now, people have two standards. Now, the second God is disappearing and belief in the Third God has not yet been established.

In church, they still preach creationism — God molded man. In school, however, teachers teach that everything that lives is a result of the natural process of evolution and not the result of the work of a supreme being created by humankind. Many people are in absolute confusion because they are learning double standards, and they believe in the theory of evolution when it is convenient for them and in God when it is convenient for them.

There are many double standard people in every corner of this society. They are so smart — they can make people believe in creationism in one place, and in another place, they can make people believe in evolution. Some of them are very successful when they choose to act two-faced. Accordingly, many people who believe in one truth and are honest and straight are sometimes not successful in society and become losers.

These two-faced people state one thing, but they do another — sometimes, they act like they are nature protectionists, but they are actually nature destroyers. Society has become so messy and confusing because there is no stable set of beliefs. Double standards never last long, like in the seasons, the transition between winter and spring, when nighttime freezes and daytime melts the ice, cannot last forever.

The human brain cannot believe in two truths — a person cannot believe $2 + 2 = 4$ and $2 + 2 = 6$ at the same time. Some double standard, sleazy people act like they can believe two truths at the same time. This sleazy kind of behavior cannot work in the information age — everyone can find out easily what he is doing. The main tool in information society, the computer, cannot have two truths at the same time; no one can input data into the computer along with other data at the same time.

There are many other people who are searching for a new ethic and would like to have ethical standards that meet the new paradigm. We must find the new ethical and moral system of the new God.

In the next century, the current trend of moral confusion will be changed because God will change. If God changes, the commandments change. But, the Third God does not have commandments. The Third God does not speak directly to the people, neither through himself nor through angels. The only way people can discover the commandments of the Third God is through observing and gathering information about the functioning of the universe, the earth, human society, and the rest of nature. Only through careful observation can the basic principles in nature be comprehended.

The first law is: *the world constantly expands.*

The universe keeps expanding, and so does man's thinking and activity. The human community must naturally keep expanding.

So, anybody who wants to stop the expansion of community or tries to shrink the community is acting against the principles of the Third God — the earth.

If some people dislike the federal government because the government collects too much taxes or for other reasons, and if, for instance, they try to build a separate, smaller republic of Texans, they are against the law of the earth because they are trying to create a smaller community in an expanding world.

If some people do not like black people, and they want to have a community only for whites, then they are acting against the law of the universe.

If some Jewish people want a nation only for Jewish people, then they are also working against the law of the earth because they must expand their vision along with the rest of the expanding universe and embrace all humanity.

If any nation feels comfortable, enjoys economic prosperity, and does not want other ethnic groups living together because they have different cultures and traditions, and if they close their borders to other people in order to stop the human community from expanding, they are acting against the law of earth.

If some people do not like animals and want a man only society, they are acting against the law of earth.

If any ethnic group feels superior to another ethnic group, they are acting totally against the law of the earth.

The second law is: *time is future oriented; time never stops moving forward.*

Time on earth never goes back to the past on earth; time must head towards the future. Time flows from yesterday, to today, to tomorrow, and time never goes from tomorrow to today and finally to yesterday.

There are many people who are not happy with many aspects of the present time — either they are dissatisfied with the economic, political, and cultural chaos in the present era or they are nostalgic for the past.

Those who are interested in the past are trying to revive old cultures, customs, and old systems in human society — like some conservatives in the United States, like some leftover communists, and like some Muslim fundamentalists who want the world to revert to the past — and are against time and the law of the earth.

Religious conservatives would like the world to return to the religious lifestyle prevalent in the past. Communists saw the turbulence in democratic society and would like to return to a communist society. Muslim fundamentalists who believe that modern Western culture is rotten, corrupted, poisonous, and contaminates the heart of younger generations throughout the world want to go back to the good old times when everyone was religious and strict and women had to wear veils.

There is another group of people who want to stop time because they like the present condition very much and are trying to stop evolutionary change. They do not want to go to the future. Many political leaders, business leaders, and rich powerful people belong to this category because they want to maintain their present prosperity and fear losing their fortunes.

All of these people are violating the law of the earth that time must move forwards to the future. There is no way to go back to the past or stop moving towards the future.

Since time always goes to the future, people who do not think about the future consequences of their present actions are violating the law of the earth. If a person lives only for his own convenience and pleasure and does not think about the consequences of his actions for future generations, he is breaking the law of the earth.

The third law is: *gravity is the basic energy of the earth.*

The earth is organized with many different elements of different character. Some are heavier, some are lighter, some are larger, and some are smaller. Iron is heavy, and carbon is lighter. Sand is small, and a rock is larger. Because of gravity, all of these different kinds of elements stick together and have formed the earth, the only planet with existing life in the universe as far as we know now.

There are many different kinds of people in the world, and some are large, and others are smaller, some are black, some white, some are intelligent, and others are ignorant. Some are stronger and others are weak. Some are old while others are young, and some people are healthy while others are sick.

These various kinds of people stick together and form a community.

Even though some people do not like to live together with other kinds of people, we still have to belong to human society. Nobody can live away from human society in complete isolation from others. Even if a person does not like other people because of ethnic differences, cultural differences, class differences, differences in education, personality traits, and other differences, no one should leave the diverse human community on the earth.

This is the law of the earth.

Gravity plays another big role in the formation of the earth, and, in the same way, in the formation of human society.

Before the earth became solid, gravity pushed down high places and pushed up lower spots and formed a fairly even surface across the earth. On earth, there are high mountains and deep valleys, but in general, the earth is mostly flat.

If there were no gravity, mountain peaks would be millions of feet high.

Naturally, the bottoms of mountains would be millions of feet lower, which makes a huge gap. Because of gravity, the earth is a rounded and a relatively flat surface.

There are many people in the world who earn less than one dollar a day, and there are some people who make a million dollars a day — this is not only unfair, it is also against the will of the earth.

There are mountains and low valleys on earth, so there must naturally be rich people and poor people. But there should not be one person making a million dollars a day while other people are barely making one dollar a day! The tremendous gulf between the rich and poor and strong and weak must be harmonized with the will of the Third God; under the horizontal paradigm, the gap must become much more fair and more even than in vertical society.

In communist society, everyone works and everyone gets paid the same — that is against the will of the earth, too.

That is, the earth is not perfectly flat like the surface of a mirror, and there are many high places and low places. Earth is not as smooth as a billiard ball and looks more like a golf ball with its bumpy surface.

Other species such as birds and animals possess an incredible difference in size.

A hummingbird weighs only five ounces, and, in contrast, an ostrich weighs one hundred pounds, which is a tremendous difference in size.

Some fully grown small dogs weigh only one pound, while other dogs can weigh up to two hundred pounds when full grown.

Some monkeys only weigh several pounds while some gorillas weigh around five hundred pounds.

The largest people on earth, sumo wrestlers, weigh no more than five hundred pounds, and the pygmies in Africa are never less than fifty pounds in weight. These facts might indicate that the earth does not allow a huge difference between the sizes of human beings.

Some people eat enormous amounts of food and get fat, often over three hundred pounds, while other people, even children, have emaciated bodies as skinny as a pencil — that is against the law of the earth.

Anybody who makes more than the amount of the common person and leads a lavish lifestyle that wastes natural resources is against the law of nature. If they are using ten times more products than the common person, they are harming nature and are against the law of the earth. In human society, there must be some differences, but there should not be a polarization between rich and poor — extremes are the exception in nature.

Because of the force of gravity, people must stick together and will live a fairly even life.

The fourth law is: *plurality exists on earth.*

There is daytime, and there is nighttime, nature and people, men and women, high and low, birth and death, young and old, and success and failure. In mathematical terms, we have positive and negative, plus and minus. Each of these different characters depend on each other and compete with each other.

One side gains, and another side must lose.

If daytime gains one more hour, then nighttime loses one hour.

If people gain more, nature loses.

If men gain more, then women lose.

But if one side is too strong and keeps gaining more, then the other side, which is weaker, will necessarily lose everything and disappear.

If one side disappears, naturally the other side will disappear.

If there is no woman, eventually there will be no man either.

If people keep gaining more, there will be no nature left on earth.

If there is no nature, there will be no people on earth.

People must make harmony with nature in order to survive on this earth.

The law of evolution is the most important fact for all of humankind — because of evolution, human beings were created and evolved until the present times.

Life began at the bottom of the ocean with tiny species. Because of heavy pressure under the weight of the ocean, the small species could not move freely — there was almost no freedom.

Because of the dark and murky water at the bottom of the ocean, these species could not see — no visibility.

These species lived in a very closed society because there was no visibility and no freedom.

Now, humans have grown into a species with an average weight of one hundred and fifty pounds. Humans live under a sky much clearer than the dark bottom of the ocean, and we have a long-distance vision. We are also much more free to travel all over the world and can even reach space.

These facts indicate that evolution leads to more freedom, more fairness, more opportunities, more opulence, and more clarity in society.

Any society which has less freedom, less clarity, fewer opportunities, and less fairness — this society is less evolved from the viewpoint of evolution.

The communists say that communist society is the most advanced society because it is more fair than any other society on earth — everyone gets paid the same. Maybe they are correct, but it is not a right way to evaluate a society with a small portion of evolution. Communist society may be fairer than democratic society, but it is not as free, as open, and as opulent as democratic society.

Communist society is a very closed society controlled only by the members of the politburo and cadres of the Party, and common people do not have much information about most policies, which are, for the most part, made behind closed doors.

Because of the control of the media by the Communist Party, people do not have a clear vision of society. So, from an evolutionary perspective, communist society is one step less evolved than a democratic society.

There are some other nations whose system is much less evolved from an evolutionary perspective than democracy — systems ruled by tyrants, military dictators, and corrupt politicians.

People who believe in less evolved systems are violating the law of the earth. The fifth law states that *societies must become freer, more evolved, more expansive, and develop towards future progress.*

These are the main five laws of earth that people must believe in in the future in order to live in harmony on earth.

The most religous and ethical people will follow and recognize these laws of the earth. If a person desires to be successful in the next century, that person must be more open-minded, have a large and broad vision, and be more fair to other people.

People will not indulge in racism or prejudice in the next century.

Some of the ethical and moral beliefs from the first and second kunmady will remain, not as a commandment, but just as common sense, such as do not steal, do not rape, and do not kill other people. The most ethical and moral activity is protecting the Mother Earth, and no matter what status a person has, they will desire to protect the earth if they are a spiritual and religious person.

The earth is the mother of all humankind and all natural species, and mothers give birth to every living person. No one chooses to be born from their mother; maybe God decided that a person is born from their mother.

Naturally, of course, a good mother should educate her children well, and naturally, all children have an obligation to love, protect, and take care of their mothers — especially when she is weak and old.

There are some parents who do not treat their children fairly and are even oppressive or abusive to their children. These are bad parents, but it does not mean that children of bad parents must become bad sons or bad daughters, too. Even though the parents did not treat the children right, the children of those bad parents can help their parents when they are sick and weak. These children are the most ethical and moral children in the civilized society of Harmonism and will be respected.

Even animals love their offspring, and some species sacrifice their life for their offspring. But, there are no animals in the world that take care of their parents when their mothers get old — only human beings can do that on earth.

Taking care of parents when they are sick and old is a sign of human identity, human dignity, and is a moral and ethical virtue distinguishable from other animals. In Harmonism society, where people and animals can live together with the same right to survive, taking good care of parents will be called *moshigi*. In the next century, anyone who does not believe in moshigi and neglects their parents when they are sick and old will be treated as an immoral and unethical person who lives like an animal.

Several years ago, in one hot summer in Chicago, several hundred old people died because of hot weather, and some of them were found weeks later after they died because they did not have contact with their children. We do not know if these parents were good people or not, but we definitely know their children, if they had any, were bad sons and daughters.

People who do not respect their parents and do not know whether their parents are dead or not will be treated very harshly by society. Those people who go to church every Sunday and donate some money for charity or are involved in some community activities, but do not have contact with their parents, do not call their parents, and do not visit their parents for months or even years will not be considered moral and ethical people.

In the next century, people will evaluate how much a person takes care of their family.

In modern society, if a person gets old and physically weak, then they usually retire from social activities. Retired people are often treated as useless — most old people are sent to homes for the elderly. Most people in society do not value older people — they are treated like broken-down cars or out-of-order refrigerators. Old people cannot do the physical labor society needs in most industrial jobs; they are not as productive as younger laborers and fall behind. In modern industrial society, they almost become useless figures in society.

Under Harmonism, there will be many jobs older people can do — most of the work will not require strong muscles. Even when physically weak, they can continue to work if they wish. The older people can use their professional knowledge and experience to consult and teach the younger generation and will be valuable in many areas of society. Older men and women can advise the younger generation about how to protect nature, how to revive dying trees, and how to tame animals that come to homes. They will advise younger generations how to harmonize with other people — how to maintain a healthy relationship with people with difficult or abnormal personalities. The younger generation will come to them every time they have problems in order to get good advice for their own well-being. Older men and women will be respected as good teachers and advisors who have much experience in life and society.

But, in the next century, when people get old, are constantly sick, and are bed-ridden — when their pain is very hard to bear — some old people will end their lives voluntarily.

Under the second God, suicide is an enormous sin because human life is given by God, and no human being has the right to kill himself, no matter what their condition, no matter how weak and how much pain that person is in.

The idea that human life cannot be ended voluntarily is a consequence of the man above all belief. The belief that man is the most important — being a man is better than anything in the world — states that losing one's human life as a man is worse than anything in the world. Losing one's life voluntarily means losing manhood — remaining a human being is more important than anything else in the world.

In the next century, this belief will change. Maintaining human existence is important, but maintaining human dignity is more important. Sometimes, a man has to die in order to maintain human dignity. If he is weak, bedridden, is hurting and bothering others day and night, cannot move, and experiences unbearable agony from moment to moment while he cries for more medicine every minute, he has lost his human dignity. Some people decide to stop their life voluntarily in this case, and people will understand death is a natural part of human life.

Most people, when they face death, think of the question of life after death — is there an afterlife or not? Since nobody returns after death, even though some people claim they did, nobody knows exactly whether there is another world after this life or not. As industrial society and science have developed, many people have become skeptical towards the idea of life after death, and especially many scientists. The trend is that many people have become atheist and agnostic and believe in some scientists' denial of life after death, and this theory is based on a man almighty concept.

Atheists, agnostics, and some scientists are claiming that nothing could exist without a person's ability to perceive it through the human sensory faculties — if we cannot smell something, hear something, touch something, taste, see, and figure out something, there is no way such a world could exist. There is no world after human life because we cannot conceive of the next world.

These people's mentality is similar to the mentality of a frog living at the bottom of a deep well. In the frog's perception of the world, there is no mountain, no lake, and no ocean, and of course, no man. There is only a small sky, murky water at the bottom of the well, and that is all the knowledge they have. If someone told the frog there is another world, the frog would definitely deny it. In the same way, the scientists laughed at the people who believe they know the next world. Scientists are stating that there could not exist anything or any world beyond human sense faculty's impressions. This is a very arrogant idea.

Arrogance comes from ignorance, a short vision, and a narrow mind. In the next century, people will be much more evolved, and their sense faculties will be expanded. With new technology, they will have a broader perspective of the universe and will be able to make frequent trips through the universe. They can also research the smallest world of the atom, and then they will realize how magnificent nature is, and they will become much more humble towards nature. They will believe that there will be or must be many worlds that human beings cannot conceive of with their limited sense faculties, both in time, space, and in other dimensions.

Even now, many people believe in the existence of souls and the energy of spirit, which Asians call *chi*. And, there are many mysterious events that happen on earth even now which affirm the existence of something like chi, and even with modern science, we cannot believe that it exists yet. Some day, in the future, humankind might be able to discover the next world after death and examine its appearance. Until then, people can only be humble towards the greatness of nature and follow faithfully the law and process of nature — to have a healthy existence and make harmony with nature.

Because of the loss of the belief in the next world, morality and ethics have entirely disappeared. Since many people do not believe in life after death, they have started to believe that this world is the only and the last chance to enjoy life. People believe that they can do anything they want in order to enjoy life unless they get caught by a justice official. This belief emphasizes the present decline of moral values in the modern world.

In the next century, many people will regain the belief in the next world with the Third God, the God of nature and the earth. They do not expect to know the size and the shape of the next world like people in the era of the second Gods who believed in the devil's inferno and heaven with women in bathing suits, precious gems, and golden thrones. If people believe in the next world even though they cannot know what it will be like, they must live according to the law of the earth and follow the law of nature. They will have to live a very healthy and moral life in order to prepare for life after death.

In the next century, the most important moral and ethical principle will be to protect the mother earth, make harmony with nature, and all of humanity.

The next principle will be to take care of parents and help them through hard times and sick times.

Because of the paradigm change from vertical to horizontal, society will change from a conquering society to a harmonizing society. In the next century, people will have a much higher standard of ethical and moral codes.

Sometimes, moral and ethical standards change according to time and to place. For example, butchering and eating a cow is very unethical in India, but in America, killing and eating a cow is commonplace. A married man with more than one wife is considered immoral according to Christianity, while in Arab areas, a man with four wives under one roof is not considered to be immoral. According to modern people's morals and ethics, people in hunting society during the first kunmady were extremely cruel. They had almost no ethical and moral standards because they sacrificed people on altars in order to drink human blood as an offering to the nature gods. People in the second kunmady, the society we are currently living in, are generally greedy.

Everybody wants more and more. People want more land, more money, more property, more children, more market share, and a higher position. They are so greedy they never stop wanting more. In order to own more, they work more, they struggle hard, and they fight each other to gain more — something like the animal kingdom.

People under Harmonism do not behave cruelly like fish that swallow each other and greedily like animals fighting for food — they are humble and yield to each other.

Humility and yielding are virtues only human beings can have on earth. Animals are never humble and never yield to each other. They only yield to each other when they think they cannot win or when they are intimidated by stronger animals.

Harmonizing means to compromise and to yield to each other, so there is fairness and balance. In order to yield, a person must have a sense of humility. So, only the people who are humble deserve to live under Harmonism society. People who are cruel and greedy cannot survive in a society based on Harmonism.

Now, in the second kunmady, in the vertical society, if a person is humble and yields to others all the time, they have more chances of becoming a loser. But, under Harmonism, if a person is humble and yields, that person will be more successful. If, for example, there is a pizza party in the first kunmady, the stronger will take everything and the weaker will disappear. In the second kunmady, people will fight each other to take more pieces of pizza. In the third kunmady, people yield to each other and are generous to each other. Imagine a pizza party after a football game in an American high school where there is no cruel person who takes the whole pizza away. Students yield to each other and congratulate each other for working hard. Because everyone is smiling, laughing, and enjoying themselves, and no one is competing for more pieces, people are enjoying life and each other. A student who yields more will be the most popular in school.

Harmonism is much more civilized and has a high ethical and moral code. People have very happy lives and are more friendly to each other because of their ethics and moral practices.

JUSTICE

What is justice? People have debated about justice for a long time, from philosophers to average people with common sense, and all of them basically agree that justice is the idea that all people should be treated fairly and equally. Ever since the beginning of human history, people have never been treated equally and fairly in spite of their desire for fair treatment.

In the first kunmady, when the point paradigm existed and the strongest grabbed everything, the orders of the village chief or community chief made up the law and justice of the people. Usually, the chiefs of the community were the priests of the God that the people believed in. The chief executed justice in the name of God. People could not protest whatever the chief said and if he condemned innocent people, no one could question his authority because the chief's commands were sanctioned by God, the most powerful force in the world.

The paradigm changed and the era of man began, but still, justice was not fair towards the common people. Throughout all of historical time, the stronger, the higher, and the more wealthy have had the advantage, and the poorer, the weaker, and the lower people have always suffered miserably from injustice and inequality.

The kings in absolute monarchy possessed the divine right to rule their people, so no one dared to punish them regardless of the injustices they committed against their own people.

In feudal society, the nobles claimed almost the same right as the king, and they felt blessed by their Creator for their class. They treated the common people however they wanted - if a maid broke a fragile wineglass, she could be instantly beheaded, and even some nobles sliced off the head of a common peasant if he hadn't paid taxes on time! All of these crimes were committed because they believed God had given them the right to be superior over common people.

Everybody knows how unfair and cruel the Inquistion was during the Middle Ages. Galileo, one of the most intelligent inventors in human history, was almost beheaded because he defied the Church in the name of scientific progress.

After the Middle Ages, people became more civilized, and only by law could people get tried and punished, rather than by divine right and privilege. Equal and fair treatment regardless of class, gender, race, and status under the law is the basic principle of the modern justice system.

Even though the law in theory is fair and establishes equality among all people, in practice, the stronger and wealthier classes are much more powerful than the weaker classes and can often use the law to their own advantage. In a capitalist society, if a person has enough money, they can buy the best lawyer, and they can collect all of the witnesses and information with their money, while a poor person cannot afford a good lawyer, and they do not have time and money to get witnesses and the proper information — eventually the poor person will lose and the rich people will win in court.

That's why people say, "Money talks."

Even though the symbol of the American justice system is a scale, all the time one side is heavier and the other side is lighter — the scale seldom makes a balance.

Justice

The reason why during man's era injustice, unfairness, and inequality are so widespread in the second kunmady is straightforward — it is a man first era based on conquering and a vertical paradigm.

In the next century, justice will be done by the Third God, the God of earth.

A man can hold a baseball bat upright, which is vertical, but as soon as man lets go of the bat, the bat necessarily falls on the ground. The bat on the ground is horizontal. The second God is a vertical God, and the Third God is a horizontal God. Horizontality means evenness, equality, and fairness, and in the next century, the justice system will be much more fair, even, and equal than nowadays.

In the third kunmady, anybody who kills someone intentionally must die. No matter what kind of excuse a man has, no matter how high his class is, no matter how strong he is, and no matter how rich he is, regardless of how old or young he is, or how intelligent, that person must die. This is the law of the earth.

On the earth, if a person climbs a ten-step ladder, that person must descend ten steps. If a person descends one hundred yards into a cave, sooner or later that person must emerge from the cave by climbing up exactly one hundred yards. No matter what kind of class a person has, they must climb up in order to get out of the cave. The law of the earth treats people equally and evenly.

In the man first era, the king claimed he had the divine right to rule, and even if he killed someone, he should not be punished and executed. The noble man acted the same way, and for the same reason, he evaded justice. In a democratic society, everyone has the same divine right from God that only nobles and kings had in the past, and some people claim, if some criminals kill someone, only God can punish the criminal and humans cannot execute him for the crime he committed. In short, man cannot strip another man from his right to live.

Because of the belief in the man God, unfairness, inequality, and the gap between rich and poor happened on earth. Kings, nobles, and even the middle class evaded capital punishment, and only the poor could not avoid capital punishment.

The Third God has no exceptions — everyone is treated the same. If somebody kills somebody, they must die as a result.

Every person born on earth must die after one hundred years of life, whether they are rich or poor. Maybe some people live a little longer, and some people live shorter lives, but almost everyone dies after one hundred years of life. There are many kings and nobles who tried to live forever and evade death, but no one made it. The earth treats everyone equally in matters of life and death.

Even someone who kills another person for a good cause, or for society, or in order to protect the earth, he has to die, too. Somebody who desires to kill somebody for a good cause has to be prepared to die for that cause. Even if people might admire him as a saint or hero, still he must die because it is the law of the earth — anyone who kills somebody must die.

Any criminal who killed somebody intentionally in a cruel way, that person must die in a cruel way, too.

This practice of punishing the criminal in the same way the criminal made the victim suffer might seem to be an uncivilized way of treating criminals, like practices of torture in the Middle Ages, but it is not.

The word "civilizing" means in society: people are treated more fairly and equally without favoritism or discrimination. The victim, the poor girl, suffered and was killed, and if the criminal dies on a comfortable electric chair, the punishment is not fair. In a civilized society, the punishment the criminal receives should at least equal the suffering the victim of the crime experienced.

Sometimes, the victim's family petitions the justice system to spare the criminal capital punishment because of religious beliefs. They think that they are helping society by sparing the criminal punishment. They do not realize how much they are harming society in the long run by encouraging criminals to evade capital punishment because of the victim's sympathy. In the United States, around 30,000 people are murdered every year, and less than 30 criminals are executed every year; there should be a balance between the deaths of victims and the criminals executed in order for justice to be maintained. Justice has clearly not been done, and the present system is ruthless because it has too many ways for criminals to evade fair and equal punishment.

Another main reason people oppose the system of capital punishment is in order to support the rights of the wrongly accused criminals who receive the death penalty. Innocent people will always die and be punished for crimes they did not commit as an accident, but they are the exception rather than the rule, especially in the twenty-first century during the information age. Because of developed technology, it will almost be impossible for an innocent person to be executed.

In the next century, international crime will be tried by the Earth Union law and in the Earth Union court. Those who pollute and contaminate the air, the water, and the earth severely, along with international terrorists, organized criminals, drug producers, drug traffickers, and the manufacturers of biological chemical weapons, war criminals, and criminals who promote pornography on the Internet, all of them will be tried by Earth Union law in the Earth Union court. If they are convicted as guilty, they will be sent to the earth prison, which will be built on a remote place on earth, possibly above Siberia, near the North Pole.

The Earth Union police will operate in every local country in order to enforce the Earth Union law, and they will work with the cooperation of local police forces. They will collect information, investigate, and arrest criminals. Now, in the present time, if a criminal commits a crime or launders money, they can escape to Switzerland or other independent nations. It will be totally impossible in the Earth Union society.

Because justice is practiced in the name of the God of man, courthouses now resemble churches. Judges wear flowing robes like preachers, and the Bible is always on a desk. Everyone has to swear according to the Bible to tell the truth on the witness stand. The rivaling attorneys and prosecutors, in order to help their clients, make long speeches that sometimes last weeks or even years in order to persuade the jury and the judge, as well as the public. The lawyers' speech resembles a preacher's sermon.

The point is that trials like O.J. Simpson's, which lasted over one year, and the Oklahoma trial, which will last over one year in length, drag on for a long time because of the legal system and prolong the victims' agony. The victims must relive the tragedy they experienced for often longer than a year in court and must live with the sorrowful memories and the agony of the incident of the crime.

In this justice system, all of the sadness, agony, and hardship of the victim's family is not considered even one iota.

Trials and punishment for criminals are for the security of society and to compensate the victim or the family of the victim for the traumatic loss, sadness, and tragedy they experienced as a result of crime. Justice ought to be done to mend their broken hearts and to help the victims lead a normal life.

Justice officials act in court like they are doing a performance, with talking, gesturing, and making long speeches. They dig out and show off all of the traumatic events at the scene of the crime time after time, which hurts, saddens, and almost tortures the victims' family by forcing them to relive the tragedy often. Professionals who are trained to be lawyers, judges, and other officials have no choice but to follow the age-old system and have very limited freedom to change the system from within.

The courtroom will totally change in the next century. Nature has a strong power to cure wounds; time is the best medicine to cure human wounds. Time passes by, and many wounds are cured, and many people forget all the pain of memories and broken hearts.

They are able to resume a normal life after the traumatic experience with time in most cases.

The earth has a strong power to cure wounds, too. In the fall, many leaves fall down and scatter all over. Wind blows them, and they gather in one place, and they are eventually covered with white snow. Rain carries away fallen leaves into the water, and eventually, they are buried in the deep lake or the sea.

Nature never digs out all of the pain of the past. Anybody who digs out other people's tragedy, sorrow, and broken hearts — basically subjecting them to spiritual torture - is against nature. The wound and the broken hearts of the victims and their family should be cured as soon as possible and not dragged on for years and years. It should not be dug out again and again.

Under Harmonism, any justice officials who cannot make good harmony and balance with the related people of the case and do not collect all information, analyze it, and make a judgment efficiently and fast enough to comfort the victim and the victim's family, will be disqualified and discredited. Nobody has a right, even justice officials, to cause more pain to the victims and the families of the victims; rather, their responsiblity to the victims is to diminish the pain they have experienced as much as possible.

In the information age and under Harmonism, the courtroom will resemble a research lab instead of a church. All the justice officials, the judge, the prosecutors, and the lawyers, they will be mostly experts or technicians in the issue of the trial; they will have the correct information about the case. Instead of long talks by the lawyer and the jurors who will have very little knowledge about criminals and the trail, there will be doctors, scientists, psychologists, environmentalists, and biotechnical engineers, and they will gather and carefully analyze scientific evidence, and they will make an informed decision. For example, if a criminal kills someone and scientists can prove the murder with objective evidence, then the judge must punish the criminal, no matter what class, gender, or ethnicity the criminal has.

The trial will be very swift, precise, and efficient, and trials will seldom last longer than one day after all information is collected and analyzed. There will be no long speeches by lawyers or long hours of deliberation by jurors. If there is information that proves the criminal killed, then punishment will be carried out.

As the information age develops, most trials will be done in cyberspace and on the Internet. Everyone who is concerned or interested in the case will be able to see the trial at home, and they can be a witness, and they can contribute their opinion, too. Trials will be much more fair and precise in the information age.

* * * * * *

In America, the strongest and wealthiest nation on earth, people are afraid to walk outside during the nighttime because of the threat of crime and violence. A few years ago one lady was killed at nighttime, at around 8 P.M., in Central Park in New York. Public opinion believed she was in the wrong place at the wrong time. She was not in the wrong place at the wrong time, and we as a people should do whatever is possible to prevent such tragic situations of human suffering.

Almost every day, in gas stations, in banks, and in stores, innocent customers are murdered callously. Almost every time someone is murdered, people say that the victims were in the wrong place during the wrong time. A public park is not the wrong place to jog, and 8 P.M. is not the wrong time to jog, and gas stations, banks, and stores are not the wrong place to be. Businesses open at night are not open at the wrong time. They were cruelly murdered because they lived under the wrong justice system on earth.

In order to bloom flowers, the snow must melt. In order to bear a new baby, the older generation must die. In order to make good citizens live freely, bad people must be restricted. Good citizens should not have to restrict their lives and freedom during the night-time because of criminals. Criminals should be restricted and must suffer punishment as a result of their actions.

In order to do so, anybody who belongs to a criminal organization or is potentially harmful to society will be confined to one place. There will be no people who will be victimized in parks at 8 P.M. because they were in the wrong place at the wrong time, and people who indulge in the wrong kind of behavior must be restricted.

Many crimes occur in vertical society because of the gap between the rich and the poor. The next reason is a consequence of capitalism — the belief that money can do everything and the basic greed prevalent under the capitalist system. Under Harmonism, the gap between rich and poor is much more fair, so people can make a modest living. Naturally, crime committed as a result of poverty will decrease.

Even if a person has millions of dollars by crime, there will be no place to hide money in, and there will be no place to spend money lavishly. All big money will be monitored, and no one can have a fleet of cars or a huge estate. It doesn't make sense to commit crime for money and go to jail. Naturally, such crime will disappear.

As the information age develops, society becomes much more clear. There will be no dark room where a person can commit crime without other people being aware of the crime.

Without a higher standard of morals and ethics and a higher level of education, no one can survive easily in an information society. People will be prevented from committing crimes, and because people will be more educated, they will not want to commit crimes, and they will be more knowledgeable. Under Harmonism, justice will prevail everywhere throughout all of society, and everyone will be treated fairly and equally, whether a victim or criminal. There will be much less crime committed and a much more free, peaceful, and comfortable society than now.

But, like on earth, there is a sunny, optimistic side and a dark, pessimistic side to every civilization. There will still be some crimes committed, and there will still be some unfortunate victims. There will be some tragedies, too. People must live with this because even the earth did not make the whole world completely even and equal — there must be mountains and valleys on earth.

Society will be so much more fair than now, and there will be much less legal cases. From the viewpoint of justice, Harmonism will be a very good society for good people, and a very harsh society for unethical people who jeopardize the well-being of others and set a poor example for the rest of society.

FAMILY

The family is the central building block of all social life in every culture in the world and throughout history. If a society does not support the family system, then the entire society is flawed. All societies developed their complex social structure from the nuclear family.

Now, families are shattered by the current social system and are in shambles. In the next millennium, one of the most crucial tasks will be to rebuild the family and renew the ties between family members. It will be much easier for families to exist in harmony because there will be much better relationships between all members of society under Harmonism, and there won't be so many economic and social pressures on the family.

Everywhere, wives and husbands are getting divorces — the divorce rate in America, the most developed nation in the modern world, is at least 50 percent. Because of divorce, families are scattered across the world, and, in many families, each member lives a separate life from other members of the family.

According to anthropologists and sociologists, in primitive societies, women were the central figure of the family; societies were matriarchal.

In gathering society, women's roles were far more important than men's roles. Women picked up nuts and fruits and peeled them, and they determined whether the food was edible or not edible. Women did this job better than men.

Men invented the bow and the arrow as well as spears, and they needed to be very strong in order to shoot arrows far into the sky towards their distant targets. They needed to be very fit in order to throw spears at buffalo and bring them home after killing them. Naturally, men's status became higher than women's status, since men contributed more to society by bringing home large prey after hunting in the plains. A patriarchal society began with the onset of hunting and gathering societies.

When agrarian society began, trees were chopped down to build houses and mountainsides were burned down. The plow was used to cultivate the earth, and trees were uprooted. The job required much strength in order to be productive. Men could do the job much better than women because they had more physical strength; therefore, in agrarian society, men enjoyed a higher social status than women.

In order to cultivate more land, more labor is needed. Women needed to produce more children, so families could have more hands to cultivate the land.

Women desired to have male children because men could cultivate the land better than women.

Then, there appeared the God of man, a God designed to meet the needs of agrarian society. The Christian God said that God created man first, and after that, woman was created second by God from one of man's ribs. The Muslim God said that man can have four wives under one roof. Buddha said, "Men only enter paradise at the end of life, and women cannot enter paradise." Women were so inferior, if they wanted to enter into paradise, they needed to transform themselves into men.

These beliefs of the second Gods formed a society based on the superiority of men over women, a totally vertical society, and because of this belief, many women have been discriminated against, have suffered, been battered, and even executed by men.

In the second kunmady, the family system has been maintained by male supremacist vertical society - from absolute monarchy, feudalism, capitalism, and late twentieth-century capitalism and democracy. There is no society in the course of three thousand years that did not assert the dominion of men over women. This is a very unfortunate fact because women are naturally more compassionate than men and balance the aggressive instincts that are usually associated with men.

Men could always do whatever they wanted in the family, and women could not complain about that. Men could have other women as concubines, mistresses, lovers, and whatever they wanted, if they could afford it. But women could not have more than one lover or another lover except for her husband. Even some societies would not allow women to marry again after their husband passed away. Men could have as many women as they wanted and could afford while their wives were still alive and healthy, but women could never enjoy the same privileges. A man who has relationships with more women than his wife is treated as a higher class and more powerful man.

In China, some emperors had thousands of court ladies in their palaces. Some court ladies did not have to share the bed with the emperor even once during their entire lifetime. They could not find any men in the palace except eunuchs who supervised the court ladies to prevent them from sleeping with other men. These court ladies, after they got old and retired, could not see any other men and remained confined in one place.

In the West or the East, almost every man who belonged to the high class had mistresses or concubines. There is no equality and no fairness in this type of society. In a household, man had total power over his wife. He had the right to divorce his wife anytime he wanted, and he had the right to bring women into his house anytime he desired. Women's role was obedience to the husband, to breed his children, and to raise them. She had to cook food, take care of the house, and do the laundry as well.

While men could enjoy a sex life outside marriage at all times, if women did the same thing, she was punished severely, and in most cases, even beheaded. We all know Hawthorne's famous book about the woman who had to wear a scarlet letter for the rest of her life for committing adultery.

As people became more civilized in democratic society and as the vertical paradigm switches to the horizontal paradigm, family values, which so far have been maintained as a strict vertical paradigm system, will start to shake and collapse. Now, in American society, the modern family system is foundering and is in very poor shape. Americans need a new vision for the next century and coming millennium of harmony between family members.

Many American women, mostly young and progressive women, could not accept the oppressive vertical family system — they could not live in such an unfair and immoral system. They could not tolerate being treated as inferiors to men, and they called this society a chauvinistic, male supremacist society. They wanted an equal relationship between the sexes instead of the vertical system between men and women. They divorced men who did not treat them as equals, and they looked for an equal and fair life in the family.

Because we are at a transition period from the vertical paradigm to the horizontal paradigm, some women have found husbands who treat them as equals instead of as inferiors. Many women have asked for equal rights with men and have even left the vertical system family. There are, however, many chauvinistic men still in the current society, and many women are not as fortunate. Many women live alone because they have not found the right partner.

Still, society is man centered and designed only for man. For single women, it is very hard to survive and live well in a chauvinist, vertical society, especially when women need to raise their own children.

In the next century, women will be superior to men in some areas, and in others, there will be more equality because, under Harmonism, men and women must make harmony.

Because of the law of the earth, women will be superior to men in some respects. If daytime keeps getting longer than nighttime, then, at a certain point, nighttime will become longer than daytime.

In the man first era, man is stronger than nature and tries to overpower the natural world, but in the era of the Earth God, nature is stronger than man. Just as men were superior to women, in the next century, in order for women's lives to improve after three thousand years of inferior status under men, women's status will become at least equal or superior to men.

It seems like nature is working towards that goal. Human society is changing and evolving now and needs women's roles more than men's roles.

Men can do a better job chopping trees, burning down forests, and destroying nature than women, but taking care of trees, maintaining green forests, and protecting nature — women can do a better job performing these activities.

Cultivating land with a plow and manufacturing heavy equipment with steel in industrial society - all of these activities man often excels in. But, collecting information, organizing and analyzing data with precision and painstaking care, programming with computers in the information age, or even performing scientific research in laboratories — women can do this just as well as men or even better.

Most of all, men have excelled at attacking weaker people, destroying villages, and conquering other nations and people with guns and tanks, but women definitely can do a better job helping poor and weaker people and supporting community programs for villages. Women are also more sensitive, more caring, and more friendly to people from other nations. These qualities are the most important qualities under Harmonism. Naturally, women will take over the driving seat of society, and men will have to go to either the passenger seat or the back seat.

In the next century, women will be the central figures of the family. Nevertheless, women will not become superpowers towering above men and children. Women, men, and children will be treated equally. No one will be above anyone else in a society based on harmony.

In some families, older people have a superior status to the younger generation. The older people make all of the decisions in the family. In other families, children are more important than anyone else in the family. Because children need a good education and because they want them to have a prosperous life, parents often become a slave to their children. All of these family values are based on a vertical paradigm, which will be changed in the next century. All members of the family will have fairly equal rights and will do their part in order to maintain the value of the family.

Divorce will decrease much more in the next century.

In the next century, in the information age, marriage will be carried out on precise and accurate information about the partner. Both sides, both men and women, will collect all of the information needed, such as health, education, career, character, hobby, and talent, and even genetic information, and will know each other's future plans as well. For example, they will know how many children the spouse will want to have, where they want to live, and where they would like to go on vacation. Based on all of this information, they will analyze the data and based on love, then, when they feel both sides match well, they will get married.

In vertical society, many marriages were not carried out according to the free will and love of both sides. Marriage was often carried out because of class and property, or money, power, and social status — all of these factors played an important role in marriage. Seldom, people married out of love or free choice on both sides.

Because of this, if one side lost either social status or money, the marriage naturally failed. If a man made a million dollars and married a woman, often she married him because he had money and power rather than from the power of love. If he lost the million dollars on the stock market, she would divorce him in a second because he was penniless.

Under Harmonism, people will marry with pure love and from free choice, and they will gather all of the information about how to survive and live well together in society. Divorce will be rare because people will have a sense of loyalty, commitment, and honesty in their relationships that does not exist in our present-day society. There will not be much of a gap between reality and the expectations of each partner. Naturally, marriage will last long and both partners will work together and help each other overcome difficulties in order to maintain a harmonious relationship.

Of course, there will be some people who do not collect enough information and who did not analyze the information about each other well. Eventually, there will be some gap between some husbands and wives, and they will end up with a divorce. But, in an information society, no one can have many divorces without leading a disadvantaged social life. Marriage is one of the most important contracts of life, and anybody who breaks that important contract many times will not be treated well in society.

Under capitalism, if some people do not manage their property well and borrow money from a bank or from other people without paying back the money and become bankrupt, they will be treated badly by society. In the information age, anybody, whether male or female, who divorces many times because of marrying based on poor and wrong information, will eventually be mistreated in society.

Now, some men who have married many times and divorced many times are sometimes even admired by some people in society as being a playboy. And, some women, especially actresses, who have married and divorced many times, are admired as a star and envied by many women. These are remnant phenomena from the vertical family system. In the next century, these men and women will be treated in the same way as people who have made several bankruptcies, and they will have to live at the bottom of society.

Sex life for men and women in families is very important, and both sides must have equal rights concerning sexual matters. The core of marriage is: both sides love each other as husband and wife. No extramarital sex should be allowed because the contract states that they love each other and are loyal to one another. Both sides must honor and keep loyal to this contract because it is part of their dignity and social reputation. As long as the marriage lasts, they must keep this promise in order to maintain dignity, virtue, and honor as civilized people.

Human beings have two important physical desires: one is the appetite for food, and the other is sexual desire. Most other species on earth, such as birds and animals, have sexual desire periodically for the production of offspring. Human beings enjoy satisfying their sexual desire, not only for producing the next generation, but also as a form of pleasure. Sexual desire must be a privilege given to humankind by the Creator or God. So, everybody has the right to enjoy a sex life, even though in the past, men alone were allowed this pleasure, and women were not allowed to have the privilege to enjoy sexual desire.

After the collapse of the vertical family system, women desired to enjoy sex as much as they want, and now, they can choose their sexual partners freely. They are now enjoying sexual freedom and are liberated from over three thousand years' oppression by men. In the past, they were abused, often oppressed, and had to listen to men's orders, but for the first time in history, they are now able to live, work, and enjoy sex however they wish without fearing men.

Liberated women call this "sexual freedom," and they enjoy it.

They are able to pick up their sex partner at any place, any-where, and anytime, if they have the desire. They pick up sex partners whenever they have the desire, just like people often pick up hamburgers anytime they are hungry. Some people just meet and have sex without each other's names and any knowledge — like in the seedy movie *Last Tango in Paris*. There is no bit of love in their relationship with each other, nor any sense of responsibility towards the other person. They don't even think of the consequences of sex.

All venereal diseases, such as AIDS and syphillis, and all of the trouble and violence between the sexes, are caused by indulgence in sexual freedom.

In other words, they call this kind of sex sexual freedom. That is not sexual freedom — that's junk sex, just like junk food.

Sexual freedom must be free from everything — from money, from power, from disease, and from fear of consequences — and must be an expression of intimacy and responsibility. In the next century, under Harmonism, sex life will be based on information and will be very healthy, comfortable, and intimate. People will find out everything, and no one will want to have an unhealthy, ignorant, and careless partner, and they will want the relationship to be based on pure love and free choice. They will want to have a reliable, supportive, and friendly partner who is intimate and caring.

Some people will marry and make a family, and some will choose to stay single, but both of them will have a much more free, equal, healthy, and friendly relationship with people. In the next century, the family system will be much more secure and stable because of the horizontal paradigm, and no one will act like a dictator in the household. Each member of the family will yield to each other, compromise with each other, support each other, and depend on each other.

TREASURE AND FASHION

Just as spring always follows winter and brings a new paradigm that turns barren wood stalks into lush, leafy trees and snow-covered ground into beautiful fields of green grass and colorful flowers, the new paradigm of the Third God will completely transform the landscape of mankind's mental, emotional, intellectual, and spiritual values, including what society values as treasures.

From the beginning of the earliest civilizations, humankind has always been attracted to the beauty found in the natural world — brightly colored feathers, vivid flowers, rosy sunsets, silky animal skins, sparkling gems, and precious metals — and either wants to possess these treasures or incorporate them into their daily lives as objects of art or personal decoration. So, whether for religious reasons, cultural traditions, or personal aesthetics, people throughout history have always been "accessorized." It's an intriguing urge — and one that is uniquely human. No one sees birds adorning their feathers with colorful flower petals, deer attaching bright feathers onto their antlers, or fish wearing rings of festive coral around their fins.

But as with everything else, as civilization has evolved, the items valued by different societies as treasures have changed with the times, as well as the reasons why particular objects were so greatly valued.

Ancient tribes who believed in the nature gods would make elaborate necklaces and bracelets out of the body parts of their slain enemies — usually bones or teeth. Tribal jewelry symbolized the power, strength, and authority of the wearer — the bigger the necklace and the more bones or teeth used, the more powerful the tribal chief and the more "successful" he was as a leader and a warrior. Bones were also valuable for their industrial use, as it were, because tribes could fashion tools and weapons from skeletal remains.

The shamans had beautiful feathered headdresses, along with bracelets, and decorative clothes adorned with many shells. Often, the leaders of tribes wore bracelets of turquoise with images of eagles, and the more precious stones the leader had, the more powerful he was among his people. The more elaborate the art and costumes the leader possessed, the more authority the leader had among his people.

In the second paradigm based on conquering nature, society began to treasure objects found in nature as prized possessions of the ruling class, from ornate gemstones to beautiful silky coats of the tiger, jaguar, and leopard. Pieces of ivory from the tusks of elephants that could be carved into delicate figurines were sought after by the wealthy and elite.

The more exotic and the more rare the object, the greater its appeal and the higher its value, which is why precious stones and metals, so rare and so beautiful with their rich, dazzling colors, but hidden deep in the ground and not easily accessible, were valued by society above all. Usually, only the rich and powerful could afford to buy jewelry and other objects made from these resources on earth, so these treasures of society also became symbols of success and power. Now, instead of using feathers and bones, kings had elaborate crowns made, filled with priceless gemstones because the more jewels in the crown, the greater the stature of the king.

Even after monarchies began to vanish, though, the desire to possess these treasures only increased and remained an obsession of society. If a person owned a gold trinket or a bauble with an emerald or ruby in it, that meant he was that much more important, that much more successful than the average person who could not afford to own precious resources.

But, as the world's population grew, the demand outgrew the supply. In order to satiate the public's appetite for the treasures of the earth and quench man's desire to possess these beautiful stones and metals, one of the greatest threats to the earth became a booming business — mining. The amount of devastation caused by mining is almost unimaginable when one considers that in order to obtain one single ounce of gold, a full quarter acre of land must be destroyed, with the surrounding habitats ruined for all the plant and animal life in the area. The search for diamonds and other precious gemstones has resulted in entire mountains being hollowed out, and all of this damage to the earth has been done for stones that do nothing to advance human knowledge or health and have fascinated humankind only because of their stunning colors.

Jacqueline Kennedy, the beautiful First Lady of the United States, wore a leopard coat and proudly displayed her coat to the news media, and immediately, leopard coats became a fashion for women in upper-class society who wanted to impress their peers. In the next year, more than 3,000 leopards were slaughtered on earth to meet the rising demand for leopard coats, and the leopard soon became an endangered species.

People have raped, mined and abused the natural resources of Mother Earth in search of societies' treasures, and in the process, many innocent and unsuspecting species have had their natural habitats destroyed. Some species were totally wiped out because of their fur or their valuable hides, and human beings, without any civilized sense of compassion for weaker species, destroyed them and took adavantage of them in order to satisfy their own personal vanity. Because of all the destruction of the earth for the acquisition of precious treasures and commodities, the survival of all species on the planet and of humankind as well is now threatened, and we have encouraged a morality that places personal vanity over disappearing wildlife, ego over land conservation, and status over resource preservation. Some people decorate their rooms and offices with ivory, trophies, tiger heads, stuffed grizzly bears, big deer antlers, and marine fish in order to prove how macho they are.

How can we possibly believe we are acting in accordance with God's will when science and technology have given us more than enough information to prove that the earth's limited resources are disappearing at a dangerous rate, that mining is so devastating to land and habitats that they are completely destroyed, and that the destruction of the earth's fragile ecosystem poses a potentially deadly risk for all life on the planet?

If we truly value natural treasures, then we must fight to preserve them. Humankind has been stripping the earth for so long, the balance might never be regained, but at least more imbalance can be prevented. Just as modern man will not allow his neighbor to cannibalize the family across the street, believers in the Third God will not allow their neighbor to destroy the earth just so he can have a pretty ring or necklace to wear.

But it's such an ingrained part of our daily life that the biggest problem is making people aware of the destruction and changing their mind-set. They do not realize that the simple act of buying a gold necklace in a shopping store promotes the continued destruction of the earth.

For example, no one would ever see an animal protectionist wearing a leopard skin coat or wearing an ivory bracelet because it would scream hypocrisy — at least a person with common sense would realize that one cannot support animals and wear ivory bracelets at the same time. Nor has anyone seen any human rights activist sporting a lovely human bone necklace, which would call the sincerity of their ethics into question. But it's quite common to see "environmentalists" wearing rings, necklaces, earrings, bracelets, and other jewelry made of gold and silver, often studded with precious stones.

The very people who are supposedly the most concerned with the earth are wearing jewelry that has resulted in the destruction of acres and acres of nature.

While their hearts may be leaning in the right direction, environmentalists who aren't willing to forego their own vanity or only want to protect certain parts of the earth are just as much a part of the problem as the mining company who hires the bulldozers to carve the life out of the land. To say with the pleasing sounding words, "I want to save the earth," while acting against the idea of saving the earth in practice is a lesson in human hypocrisy.

The quest for gold has probably caused the most destruction from mines on the entire earth. Not only has gold been treasured as a symbol of success and wealth since the days of the ancient pharaohs of Egypt, gold is also used as the basis for our modern system of money — governments gauge their worth according to the gold standard. In every country, tons of gold bars are kept in maximum security vaults. But, in order to get all of that gold, millions of acres of land had to be destroyed. Habitats have been ruined, plants uprooted, and animals displaced. The gold standard, quite simply, is the mastermind of destruction.

The only way we can stop the destruction is to adopt a new morality which will change our attitudes about economic power and wealth. Just as human bone jewelry is no longer seen as a symbol of power and strength, but as a symbol of barbarism and cruelty, gold will no longer be seen as a symbol of wealth and success, but as a symbol of corruption and destruction.

After the new paradigm changes society's attitudes and ethics, people will recognize that mankind's long-standing obsession with gold and other precious stones and metals has posed a threat to the natural world. People the world over will be morally compelled to stop buying and trading in gold, which will cause in turn the value of gold to plummet and render the Gold Standard obsolete.

As mentioned earlier, earnings will be paid in units stored in computer data banks and cash will disappear. When that happens, a new measure of a nation's wealth and economic strength will emerge, based not on how much gold a country has in its vaults, but on how much information its citizens have and how well they use the knowledge gleaned from that information to maintain harmony with the earth, including a commitment to protect nature's treasures from depletion.

The point is not that gold shouldn't be used for any purpose — there are many medical and industrial uses for gold that are important to man's interests. But once people stop using gold as a personal treasure, there'll be ample gold already in circulation to fulfill those needs.

Nor at issue is the human desire to surround ourselves with beauty or to own objects of value, but how we satisfy those cravings and whether our pursuit of possessions comes at too great a cost to nature. In addition to our unique ability to appreciate the magnificence of color, God also gave people the gift of creativity, so as mankind evolves and our morals change, society will adopt and conceive of new treasures — artful creations made from synthetic materials that are just as stunning and durable as gold and diamonds, with colors and designs that please both the eye and the soul.

It's also quite possible that some of the most prized treasures of the next century won't even come from the earth, but from humanity's exploration of the universe, with polished stones brought back from Mars and other places becoming the diamonds of tomorrow. But everyone will know that the treasures of the past cannot be obtained without robbing the earth of her rarest and most precious resources.

As time changes, fashion changes as well. The basic fashion of the first kunmady is the string. Everything was made from animal hides, and strings dangled from the sleeves and the hems of jackets — even hats had strings on them. As we see with the American Indians' clothes, the more strings the clothes had, the greater the status of the person who wore them.

In the second kunmady, the basic sign of fashion is the button. People can now see the portraits of nobles who wore coats with many buttons.

The trend is still there — men still wear tuxedoes with golden buttons on their jackets. Some expensive hotels have their bellboys wear coats lined with ornate golden buttons on both sides in order to impress their customers. Sometimes, people can see the top executives of large corporations with many unnecessary buttons on both sides of their suits in order to show off to the public.

In the third kunmady, no one knows how fashion will change yet. But people will not wear many strings on their clothes, and there won't be many buttons either to show off rank or class. Fashion will be simple and unique — already many young people wear simple T-shirts with designs on them and slogans, such as "I love all animals."

In the next century, fashion will be more creative, colorful, artistic, and unique. People will not wear clothes or use items that result from the destruction of the earth and nature because everyone will respect the earth as the most important treasure humankind possesses.

CULTURE

Culture is the most important part of human society. A society without any culture resembles the animal kingdom. Only human beings can create culture and enjoy culture.

Many cultures originated from and were influenced and dominated by the idea of God. In primitive societies, singing and dancing rituals in front of altars were ways of pleasing God. The Olympic festival comes from Mount Olympia, where the Greek god Zeus came from. During the last part of the first kunmady, older civilizations in human history had unique cultures, like Greece, Rome, and Egypt, and their flourishing arts were a sign of their greatness.

Even during the second kunmady, most culture was related to the idea of God — the paintings, sculptures, music, and literature centered around religion. Next to God, culture was influenced by the kings, the nobles, and rich people, and they controlled the arts. Most artists worked for kings and nobles and could barely make a living. Even though they created great art, which is admired even now as a human legacy, their pay was very low. Without a patron or support, they could not create art. Some of the most beautiful and exceptional artistic masterpieces created during the Renaissance could not have been made if patrons had not supported Renaissance artists financially. Even the opera and other musical concerts were performed for the nobles and the wealthy.

In capitalist society, money plays a major role in cultural performance and production. All cultural events need money to be materialized, and without money, some artists who have talent cannot create good art or perform in public. In most cases, they need financial sponsors. In other words, the vertical paradigm makes it difficult for artists to survive because everything revolves around money and power. People who have more money, power, and control in society have a much easier time creating art and playing sports. People who are poor at the bottom of society have difficulties sharing their talent and skill with the public if they are artists.

As the vertical paradigm is fading away and the horizontal paradigm is starting to prevail now at the end of the twentieth century, some people who have come from lower classes in society have had the opportunity to show their talent to the world. There are many successful sports stars, musicians, and movie stars, and even some writers, who are now at the top of the cultural world - their success would have been unimaginable in the last century.

In the next century, in the new information society, the environment of the cultural world will go through a major change, just like other areas.

Now, because of the importance of money, almost all people spend most of their time earning more money. In other words, moneymaking is the major activity that humankind is engaging in now, but people in an information society will not have to work longer hours to make money and will naturally have plenty of time to enjoy culture.

Culture is not dominated or controlled by power or money because of the new technology. Without huge sums of money, anybody who has talent can create art that they like. If an artist has a good talent at painting, he can show his paintings without renting an expensive gallery by displaying them on the Internet to the public at a very low cost. Any writers who want to publish books because their work is so unique can still send it everywhere and to everyone on the e-mail so the public can have the opportunity to read it. Creating and organizing dramas and movies will cost much less because of new technology, no one will have to travel across the whole world to shoot a movie. A film producer will be able to do most of his work in cyberspace.

Almost anyone who has talent in the cultural field will easily have the opportunity to create and perform to the public without a patron or a sponsor. People do sports, arts, and other cultural activities because they love and appreciate what they do — they don't do it only for the money. Since Harmonism is a horizontal paradigm, there is not much of a gap between upper-class artists and lower class artists. Now, in our global vertical society, some movie stars make millions of dollars while some undistinguished actors can barely pay the rent. In sports, only upper-class sports figures make large sums of money, and the other less recognized sports figures have a very hard life. Even if top movie stars make millions of dollars, there is no place to spend that kind of money under Harmonism. They cannot have several houses on the beach and huge estates in the mountains like movie stars in vertical society. If the public knows they are greedy and asking for more money, they will be treated as a menace to Harmonism, and they will lose all of their fans.

There will be no money from endorsing merchandise in commercials, which is now the major financial source for the top entertainers and sports stars under the vertical paradigm. Now, some people buy some products advertised by celebrities. When they want to buy sneakers, some people choose the brand of sneakers endorsed by their favorite sports star. That's why some brands of sneakers, which are manufactured in Indonesia for only fifteen dollars, can sell in the American market for one hundred and fifty dollars, and the entertainer who endorses that brand of sneakers receives a large sum for promoting them.

In the next century, however, people will not depend on information given by the movie stars or sports stars. Consumers will be able to get much more broad information about the brand of sneakers, such as the type of material, the percentage of each material used in the production of the sneakers, and the wages of the laborers that produced the product. In the information age, all merchandise must have a label with detailed information about the production of the product, the materials used, and consumers will buy according to that information. If celebrities try to advertise products in the information age in a glamorous fashion and the manufacturers of the product do not provide consumers with detailed information, they will not be able to convince consumers to buy this product because consumers will only buy products with accurate information on their labels.

As cyberspace develops, there will be many intelligent, very sophisticated productions of culture. There will be many kinds of exchanges between cultures on the Internet — indigenous cultures will share their knowledge with artists in large cities. Everyone will be able to communicate with each other and exchange ideas through information technology.

In the second kunmady, most of the artistic subjects were human beings — statues of Buddha, images of Christ and the Virgin Mary, the rich and nobles, and sculptures of human beings. Many paintings are only man centered — many paintings are only portraits. But, under Harmonism, there will be a new celebration of nature and of harmony between human beings and nature. Many artistic creations will venerate nature because the earth will have gained a new place in the human imagination.

Culture will be a major part of human life, and many people will have time to devote their lives to art in all of its aspects — photography, painting, film, poetry, fiction and nonfiction writing and plays. Cultural activity, along with scientific acitivity, will be an important feature of human existence in the twenty-first century, and, instead of occupying their lives with making money, people will enrich themselves with the arts.

POPULATION

During the era of the first God, many people already lived in permanent communities, a change of lifestyle made possible by a revolutionary discovery — farming. Once people could control the land better and produce food consistently, the entire course of civilization changed completely. Agriculture was the single most decisive factor that made it possible for humankind to develop an advanced civilization with a complex social structure.

Once there was a reliable food supply, it was possible for larger groups of people to establish more permanent settlements and abandon a nomadic lifestyle. The solitary bands of hunters and gatherers that traveled across the plains hunting after buffalo settled down and formed villages at the beginning of agricultural society. With people settled in one spot, population increased, there were more people to farm the land, and extra crops were cultivated. With a food surplus, a community could support a variety of workers who did not farm for a living, which meant more people were available to perform different tasks and new jobs were created, which in turn led to the development of a more complex social structure.

All of the ancient civilizations probably developed in much the same way, regardless of regional and climatic differences. As

villages grew, it was possible to acquire more and better goods —
heavier, more durable pottery replaced animal skin gourds as con-
tainers for foods and liquids, cloth could be woven from wool and
flax, permanent structures could be built using imported wood,
brick or stones, and eventually the first cities appeared.

All of this development occurred because man figured out that
a seed planted in the ground will grow and produce food for an
entire community.

One unfortunate outgrowth of man's advancing civilization was
warfare and the development of weapons for destruction. When
more than one tribe or village sprang up close to one another in the
same area, each would naturally compete for fishing or hunting territories or for the most fertile land to plant their crops. Each community, regardless of size, had their own identity and, in many
cases, idolized different gods, with each side believing their god was
stronger. In order to ensure their own survival, as well as to increase
prosperity, tribes and villages would attack each other and whoever
had the strongest god, won — at least, that's what people believed a
victory meant.

The vanquished members of the weaker god's community
would then be sacrificed as a way to thank and honor the winning
god and acknowledge its strength and dominion. Those who were
spared the knife or being burned alive became slaves for the rest of
their lives.

Some people voluntarily sacrificed themselves for the well
being of their own tribe in order to please the terrifying gods whenever there was a drought and famine in the land. They wanted the
sun to shine, so they sacrificed themselves on slippery blood-cov-
ered altars in front of an assembly of villagers, and the number of
people sacrificed, including women and children, increased to
almost unthinkable numbers if the drought remained in spite of
sacrifices and offerings.

While studying the ancient Aztec and Mayan civilizations in

Central America, archaeologists unearthed a grisly discovery — the bones of thousands of sacrifice victims who had been slaughtered as an offering to the sun god and whose deaths were recorded on ancient ceremonial stones. The scope of the killing is hard for modern minds to fathom. At the dedication of the great Aztec pyramind temple in Teotihuacan, 20,000 captives were killed in a single ceremony and blood spilled everywhere.

A member of Cortes' expedition described finding a skull rack in the main Aztec square that contained 136,000 skulls. There were also additional huge mounds of skulls and five smaller racks of skulls. The practice of human sacrifice became so widespread that ritual sacrifice became a full occupation for members of some communities because it was a central part of their particular cultures.

While the sheer quantity of sacrifice victims make the Aztec and Mayans stand out in stark contrast to other cultures, human sacrifice was a fact of life in nearly every culture and corner of the globe, albeit on a much smaller scale, which is why most of the evidence of this common practice has been buried or destroyed over the eons. The custom is even mentioned in the Bible during the story of Abraham, who is asked by God to sacrifice his only son, Isaac. But right when Abraham is going to stab the boy, God intervenes and saves Isaac. Unfortunately, very few others were spared the knife once chosen to give their lives up in order to please an angry God.

Even though we know that early man endured strenuous living conditions, food shortages, and suffered from natural disasters that happened with no warning, there were still plenty of people on earth. While we don't have any way of proving with any degree of certainty the world population during the first kunmady because there was no official record keeping, scientists have estimated that the human population during the era of the nature gods ranged anywhere between five to fifty million.

Whatever the world population was at the beginning of the first kunmady, it is quite possible that population began to decline as the centuries wore on due to the constant increase in human sacrifices, cannibalism, and slavery — worldwide, daily practices that resulted in massive fatalities and bloodshed that otherwise would never have occurred. We cannot prove that population decreased with human sacrifices, but logically, it makes sense, since human sacrifices happened so often.

The paradigim of the second God promotes the gospel that man is important above all else on earth, and therefore, nature exists only at his disposal. The practices of human sacrifice and cannibalism disappeared as soon as man was revered as the highest, most spiritual, and most evolved creature in all of creation, even though slavery, an equally uncivilized custom, would take much longer to become socially unacceptable. Human sacrifice was unquestionably barbaric during the era of the second God.

The paradigm shift spurred other social changes, including a dramatic global increase in population — not so much because of agriculture, but because of the new interpretation of God's will. The new credo was more, more, more — more power for humankind, more dominance over nature, more material goods, more money, and more people. There were practical reasons to want an increase in population because countries wished to expand their own civilization, cities were developing, and people felt they would become stronger if they had more numbers.

Religious leaders told their faithful that it was God's will to have lots of children, so the number of believers would grow and thereby make the religion stronger.

As the agrarian age continued to develop and evolve in the second kunmady, the more children a person had, the more "hands" to help work in the fields, which meant more land could be cultivated, which in turn meant more crops could be raised, which meant in turn more money could be made, and finally which in turn meant the overall prosperity of the family, villages, and nations could be increased with each extra person... more is always better.

It was politically and economically pragmatic for nations to encourage population growth in order to fulfill short-term goals of land acquisition or to protect land they already controlled. More people led to a bigger, stronger army which increased a country's chances of being victorious in warfare. During World War II, both Germany and Japan urged their citizens to have many babies, and the Japanese government went so far as to offer financial rewards and patriotism medals to women who responded to the call for more children.

Since people believed that the earth was here solely for human convenience and benefit, societies and cultures all over the world stopped worrying about appeasing nature and turned their energies toward establishing themselves against other societies and cultures. Unfortunately, humankind never stopped to consider what the ramifications of a ballooning global population might be in the future.

Currently, there are over five billion people on the earth, and some scientists estimate the world population is increasing by a million people a day, which means that early in the next century the population of the earth will double to ten billion. Because of the rapid increase in population growth, severe shortages in food, energy, and fresh water will occur throughout the earth, and many forests and natural resources will be completely eliminated from the planet.

But the increases are not evenly distributed. The rate of population growth is much slower in First World nations such as America and Canada than it is in undeveloped, economically impoverished Third World nations burdened by too many people and too few jobs. In general, the more technologically and economically advanced a country, the slower the rate of population increase.

There are some people who believe that if the world economy expands enough, we will be able to educate the people of these countries to help them get good jobs, improve their national economy, and thereby reduce the rate of population growth.

Now, if nearly six billion people — virtually every person existing presently on the planet — enjoyed the fruits of development at the same rate as the First World and bought fancy cars, built large skyscrapers, and generated huge amounts of garbage and pollution, there would be nothing at all left in nature, and the magnitude of environmental destuction would be beyond the limits of human imagination.

As long as we keep approaching the problem of overpopulation from a man above all paradigm, there can never be a workable solution to our problems of overpopulation. The problem needs to be examined from a different angle and solved using a different paradigm because no matter how the problem is looked at, the bottom line never changes — there is an absolute, finite limit to the number of people the earth can support and sustain.

In the next century, population control will be the primary policy of the Earth Union government. Population growth will never be restrained by the existing 200 or more nation states on the earth. Even thought some nations will have stabilized populations, some other nations will not be able to curb their population growth for religious, cultural, political, and economic reasons.

Scientists, researchers, sociologists, economists, and other technicians who are part of the Earth Union will study population growth and the developmental potential of the earth; they will find out how many people can live a civilized and modern life without permanently depleting the earth's resources. If the earth can sustain the population more than we have in the present, even though this may never happen, we will be able to increase population gradually, but if we already have more people than the earth can sustain in the long run, we will have to take a strong population control policy. The Earth Union government will control population in a civilized and rational way and will not force people to control population size through violence like Stalin and Hitler did to their people.

Researchers will set up a standard for how many children can exist on earth in order for the earth's resources to be maintained. Once this message is spread across the globe and educates the people of the world, if people do not meet the standard, they are unethical, immoral, and greedy. Each national government will make a goal and a policy to limit the amount of children born per year that will be acceptable to the Earth Union government's standard on population. If any government does not implement this important policy, which is perhaps the most important policy on the earth, to the satisfaction of the members of the Earth Union government, then the Earth Union government will punish, reprimand, and monitor closely that government until the policy is implemented.

Population control will be a law of the Earth Union. Any nation or organization that violates the law of the Earth Union will be tried in an Earth Union court according to the law of the earth.

In order to ensure all of the national governments of the world will follow this population policy, the Earth Union will provide tremendous financial support to each national government for educational development, for more advanced medical development, birth control, and for a cleaner, more healthy environment.

In the present time, all of the nations on the earth are spending unbelievable amounts of money — well over one trillion dollars a year — on military defense budgets. In order to kill each other and wage war with each other and destroy the Mother Earth, they spend one trillion dollars. Why can't humankind use the money to help poor people in developing nations to curb the population increase and maintain harmony with nature and Mother Earth in order to promote healthy living for all of the people of the world? If humankind spent one-tenth of the defense budget, 100 billion dollars a year, for population control, then, in less than fifteen years, the earth will easily be able to sustain the human population.

If the message about limiting family size is sent everywhere on earth, then even in the jungles of Africa and in the Himalayas, families will not have too many children because everyone will be informed about the problem of overpopulation. Birth control will be an ethical and moral virtue and will be a commitment and responsibility of each member of society. The standard will be consented to by everyone and become an everyday, common sense belief in people's lifestyle. Governments will not have to enforce strictly birth control by law because people will voluntarily follow the policy. In a city bus, no one takes up two seats in a crowded bus; everyone naturally sits on one seat. All good citizens each know how much space they can take. No one with sound common sense would take five people's seats and lie down in a crowded bus. The person would be thrown out of the bus and would be a hazard to society. In the same way, any people who have excessive amounts of children, will be treated as greedy and selfish people.

There might be some families who believe, because of their religion, people can have as many children as they want — so they want to have ten children.

In the next century, any family who wants as many children as they wish, they cannot only have ten children, they can even have a mind-boggling amount of children — one hundred children because of advances in genetic science. If such religious beliefs extend to the next century, there will be many, many families who will have countless children. This is another reason why the old second God must disappear.

Under Harmonism, people will not only make harmony with nature, but also will have to make harmony with other people, too. They will voluntarily work for birth control. The idea of voluntarily limiting the size of families has already begun to happen, at least in the most advanced developed countries. In the last century, there was a sharp decline in the number of children in the average Western culture family, and more couples than ever chose not to have any children at all. Two hundred years ago, it was unthinkable for a married couple to be childless by choice, and while it is still not the norm, couples without children are not oddities anymore.

The reason for the change is partly social, partly technological, and partly practical. We are no longer an agrarian society without machinery, so there's no need to produce a family large enough to work in the fields. Scientists have discovered effective methods of birth control, and it is very expensive to raise children. Also, to help make financial ends meet, and because of gains made by women in society, fewer women are willing to spend the most productive years of their lives at home raising children.

After centuries of oppression, women have become a prominent and undeniable social force to be reckoned with. In the third kunmady, women will finally become truly equal citizens of the world so, from a practical viewpoint, a greater number of women will voluntarily choose to remain childless and devote themselves fully to careers.

* * * * * *

Sometimes scientists and doctors, in their quest to discover the next medical breakthrough, are guilty of irresponsibility. For example, to live in harmony with the earth includes maintaining a proper balance with everything, including the lifespan of man. In the next century, it is possible that new technology may make it possible for doctors to extend the life expectancy of humans beyond the upper limits of what nature intended. Just because we can do something, does not mean we should. In the era of the Third God, people will accept that it is God's will that we accept death as necessary for the survival of the earth.

Death is a part of life and on a planet that must maintain careful population control in order to sustain its resources, unnatural extension of life goes against harmony. We should make our living years as productive and as technology and science allows, but it goes against the Third God to lengthen artificially the built-in life of humans. Just as autumn turns to winter, so too comes an end to man's life on earth.

Nor does death itself end our responsibility to the earth. Today many people continue to destroy nature after they die by buying ornate mausoleums, some of which are the size of small condos, in order to be interred. In some countries, family tombs are bigger than the family house; some caskets cost more than what some families earn in a year. But it is wrong to destroy nature just to build a shrine to the dead — the pyramids and Taj Mahal are extreme examples of grand monuments to death.

Some of our current attitudes and traditions about how we bury the dead derive directly from man's belief in the second God; specifically, the belief that there would be an actual Judgment Day when the dead will physically rise and meet their maker. In anticipation of this pending resurrection, the elite of society - kings, nobles, the rich, and the famous — spent a great deal of money on expensive coffins that would keep the body as well preserved as possible.

Even those who don't believe in some type of Judgment Day will say that burial rites are deeply ingrained in their culture and to change would be to dishonor their ancestors. But tossing virgin girls into the ocean to appease the sea god was also a deeply ingrained custom, and a new interpretation of God's will put an end to that practice and labeled sacrifice a barbaric practice. In the same way, people who believe in the Third God will consider marble caskets designed to last centuries an uncivilized practice that fails to promote harmony.

In the third kunmady, during the era of the Earth God, there will be no great pyramids built, no imposing marble mausoleums, and no permanent caskets. People who believe in the Third God know they owe the life they live to nature and harmony, and they will want to repay the earth after their death. One way to do that is by being buried in a simple wooden coffin, so that their bodies and the coffin will eventually be absorbed back into the earth and replenish the soil with nutrients that will be used to provide life elsewhere. Then, instead of concrete slabs, a bed of flowers or a young tree sapling could act as a headstone which would allow their deceased loved ones to keep in harmony with the earth even after death.

But the fact is, population control won't be possible until our attitudes about life and death change - until we realize that it is not good enough to just hold the number of people on earth at a stable level, but to actually decrease population in the next century. Until we stop believing in a man centered paradigm and put the earth first, old habits will not change. The only way to change is to accept the Third God paradigm of harmony for the benefit of the earth and all the species on it.

MILITARY

Every species finds some way of defending itself against dangerous, life threatening predators — deer have antlers and speed, tigers have claws and strength, snakes can constrict and inject venom, elephants have size and tusks, birds can fly away, and sharks have thick skin and razor sharp teeth. Compared to the rest of the animal kingdom, a human's physical attributes are rather limited — early man probably learned quickly that fists were no match against wild animals. But what primitive man did possess is one unique feature that set him apart from other species, a brain capable of complex thought and creativity, so he invented clubs and other tools, like the bow and the arrow, to help him hunt for food and protect himself and his family from predators that threatened him with extinction.

In the agrarian age, the bow and arrow was used primarily as a weapon to defend land and to conquer weaker opponents in order to acquire more land. The societies with the best weapons were the ones most likely to stay strong and powerful, so an incredible amount of time, energy, and thought were invested into developing ever more sophisticated and lethal weapons — arrows led to swords, guns, cannons, aerial bombs, nuclear bombs, and weapons of biochemical destruction.

Because the paradigm of the second God encouraged humankind to go and conquer the world around him whether the adversary was from another tribe, another culture, another country, or even from wildlife or nature, weapons were vital to fulfill that mandate and enabled humankind to become a true conqueror.

But under Harmonism, individual national militaries will be dismantled in favor of an Earth Union army, a situation similar to what happened in the United States after the Civil War when, in acknowledgement of the federal government's supreme authority, individual state militias were disbanded in favor of a national military. Unlike the United Nations' multinational peacekeeping force of today, which has limited authority, is only concerned with human political issues, and is composed of different armed forces from different nations, the Earth Union military force will be recruited from all over the world and trained by the Earth Union government and leadership with one language, possibly English. Of course, a military academy will be created to train officers for the necessary leadership and skill needed to maintain an army.

In the era of the Third god, maintaining harmony will be the moral standard of society, so any renegade country, industry, or organization that illegally destroys rain forests, ruins wetlands, dumps toxic waste, pollutes the oceans, allows illicit drug production, or fails to control population will be considered terrorists by the rest of society, who will *want* the Earth Union Government to intercede.

Suppose a company breaks the Earth Union law by releasing illegal levels of pollution into the atmosphere or water. Initially, the host country would be given the opportunity to make the company comply with pollution laws. If the home country refused or was unable to control the company through national sanctions, the Earth Union government would have no choice, but to enforce the legal process itself, either through fines, prosecutions, or, if necessary, by sending in military personnel.

But enforcement won't necessarily mean armed conflict or killing people. Although the Earth Army will be equipped with state-of-the-art weaponry, they'll also be armed with other, more constructive weapons, because in addition to trained soldiers, the military will include teachers, scientists, sociologists, and doctors who will use education, science, and technology to fight earth terrorism. Violence will be and must be used only as a last resort.

During the last century, the defense industry has become one of the largest and costliest organizations in the world, so one practical advantage of consolidating military technology and power into a single Earth Army is the tremendous amount of money saved — billions of dollars will be saved. The United States government alone spends $300 billion a year on its military technology and worldwide, the cost is many times that amount. Most rational people would say that over one trillion dollars is an absurd amount of money to spend on weapons of mass destruction while millions of children suffer from hunger and die from starvation every year, especially when a substantial percentage of the world's miltitary budget is mismanaged and cost ineffective. The money saved by an Earth Union government can be used to ease poverty, fund job programs, finance individual businesses, set up scholarships, offer technical and trade school training and promote other social programs that will improve the standard of living for all the world's citizens.

While the ideal of an Earth Army holds the promise of a better life, free societies are on constant vigil against any potential threat to their personal freedom and lifestyle, and some might fear that a madman or despot could somehow take over the Earth Army and end up controlling the world. It's natural to think in those terms because people have been conditioned by the second God paradigm that encourages man to be a conqueror.

But when our interpretation of God's will changes in the era of the Third God, aggression for the sake of personal gain will be considered immoral. Just as modern societies would never tolerate any leader who started feeding people to lions for sport again or engaged in regular rituals of human sacrifice — all accepted practices in the era of the first God - people in the third kunmady would simply never tolerate an attempted takeover of the Earth Army by a Hitleresque tyrant.

Even though the Earth Army is a military organization, it will not be based on the vertical system based on rule from the top down to the lower ranks — it will be an entirely horizontal system. Each member will have equal rights and fair treatment, and freedom to express their ideas and opinions in the system whenever necessary. There will be no rank or class, and there will be only differences in commitment only. The commander is not higher than the soldiers, but his commitment is to command the soldiers, and the soldiers' commitment is to follow the orders. But there will be no warfare for causes other than protecting the earth and promoting peace on the planet.

Under this military force in a horizontal world system, the Earth Union will maintain peace all over the world. The members of the Earth Union will stop the fighting between nations, between ethnic peoples, and religious conflicts, like the strife between Jewish and Palestinian people.

AMERICA

Since the second kunmady began with the development of agrarian society, there have been many kingdoms, many empires, and many nations and forces, and all of them have had periods of success and decline. At the end of the twentieth century, America has become the last winner of the second kunmady — the era of the conqueror.

America became the wealthiest, the strongest, and the most influential nation on earth and the most powerful nation in all of human history.

America is encouraging, pushing, and forcing other nations to adopt American democracy as the ideal form of government around the world. Most of the nations on earth are now following, copying, and learning from the American democratic political system.

The American economic system, which is called the free market economy or capitalism, has prevailed across the entire planet. American multinational corporations are present in most of the nations of the earth and are selling products across the world while collecting materials for the purposes of production.

American culture is popular all over the world, from pop music to blue jeans, computer games, Coca Cola, and fast food restaurants.

American missionaries are all over the world — deep in the Amazon, in Communist China, in the Saharan desert — and are preaching to the whole world the belief in an American God. As a result of the preachers' evangelism, in the Himalayas, in African jungles, and in Indonesia, people can see churches with crosses on them everywhere.

American military forces cover the entire earth, and nearly every place in the world has been affected by the presence of the American military. Any nation that would dare to confront America would be immediately struck down by the massive American military force.

Any nation or people on earth who is acting against American national interests, either politically, economically, militarily, religiously, or culturally, will be retaliated against or subject to an embargo, or simply intimidated by the United States.

However, not all of the people or all of the nations of the world agree with or are satisfied with American policy.

Some nations complain, blame, and protest against American policies and say that American policies are too aggressive, too oppressive, and too exploitative to the weaker nations, and they claim that Americans only think about their national interest and do not consider the welfare of people from other smaller nations.

If those nations oppressed by the Americans unite and stand against America, they would possibly be able to defeat America someday. At least, some leaders of the developing nations believe that they can unite and defeat the overpowering influence of America on the rest of the world.

These complaints from these weaker developing nations may be true — maybe Americans are too aggressive, too oppressive, too arrogant, and too selfish. But, America is the most advanced nation by the standard of the law of earth — evolution. American society is broader, with greater freedom, clearer, more transparent, more fair, more opulent, and more open than any nation on the earth, even though America has some flaws.

America is oppressive, exploitative, and conceited, and America must possess all of these qualities to be a superpower and the main leader of the earth in the era of the conqueror. Now, we are living in the vertical paradigm and the era of the conqueror, and anybody who wants to become a winner must be oppressive and place his own interest first over the interests of others. Otherwise, a country that is too giving will be treated as too naive and too generous and will not be able to maintain its power and status. Any nation on earth, even the smallest nations, who complain against American policy and attitude, once that nation possessed the same power over the world, it would run the world the same way, and perhaps even worse.

There are some people, because of their unhappiness with America, who claim that America will collapse because of the lack of moral and ethical values, the widening gulf between the rich and the poor, the increasing crime rate, senseless acts of violence and terrorism, the widespread use of drugs, and the rising hatred and antagonism between different ethnicities. But, they are wrong; they only see a small portion of Amerca — the shady part of America. They do not see the resilience and ambition that comes from the American people to fix the flaws, problems, and mistakes that haunt their society, and the drive of the American people to improve their society at any cost.

At this point, no force can defeat America from the outside and no flaws can bring down American society from the inside. Nothing can topple the greatest nation on earth, the United States, at the present time.

With one exception — only great nature can defeat and can cause the United States to collapse.

If America continues to go against the laws of nature, then, America will necessarily collapse. No matter how strong and secure America is, America will always be a small part of the natural world and the entire universe.

Rome was once the most powerful, the most wealthy, and the largest empire in human history because Rome conquered and controlled most parts of Europe. In those days, no nations could rival Rome, and Rome existed as the sovereign empire in all of Europe, just like America today.

There are many similar phenomena in ancient Roman religion and present American religion; the interpretation of God is different, but the religions of these two civilizations spread all around the world. Roman gods are derived from Greek gods, which are basically nature gods with a human form, such as Jupiter, the god of the heavens, and Apollo, the god of the sun, and many other anthropomorphic gods of nature. The Romans built Roman temples in Rome and in any place that they conquered.

The American God came mostly from European beliefs in Christianity, and the Americans made minor adjustments to the European Christian God. Churches were built all across the country, and they sent out missionaries to build the same kind of churches across the world.

Both civilizations had highly developed technology. Rome had very highly developed technology and skill, and with this technology, they could easily defeat lesser civilized tribes and nations. With their technology, they built enormous roads all over the places they conquered in order to improve their transportation and communication systems with the vanquished people. Romans brought food and clothes from the vanquished people, along with gold and jewelry and many slaves to Rome. Just like Rome, America has a worldwide communication and transportation system and brings all kinds of food, clothes, and merchandise from all over the world to its own people.

In terms of lifestyle, both Americans and Romans have had excessive diets and often lived extravagantly. The Roman citizen was economically very prosperous, and they lived very lavishly and luxuriously. They would eat until they threw up, and then, they would eat more. Similarly, in America, many Americans overeat, become overweight, and diet in order to lose the weight they gained by overeating.

Rome was so rich, so strong, and so technologically developed in almost every aspect that there was virtually no enemy the Romans could be afraid of. All of the Roman people thought the Roman Empire would last forever; no Roman would think about or even imagine the decline of the Roman Empire.

Now, Americans are so strong that no other nations with common sense would dare challenge them in a power struggle, especially after the collapse of the archrival of America, the Soviet Union.

Roman society prospered by exploiting slave labor, and almost everything was done by slaves.

American prosperity comes from conquering nature, land, trees, minerals, oil, and other materials. The American economy is based on conquering more nature, creating more merchandise made by materials from nature, and consuming more products.

Early Romans sacrificed human beings, just like the believers in the first God paradigm based on nature gods. But, eventually, they stopped performing human sacrifices, yet they still enjoyed to watch slaves fighting with hungry lions in stadiums. They loved to see human blood flowing.

Americans burned down forests and made cornfields, and almost wiped out the buffalo and other wild animals. Eventually, they stopped the massive destruction of the earth, yet still they enjoyed hunting and continued to destroy nature for their own convenience and pleasure.

Then, there appeared a new breed of people in ancient Rome, Christians.

They had different values than other Roman citizens, and they claimed that humankind was the most important species on the earth. They believed that only human beings were the children of God. So, nobody had the right to kill human beings in stadiums engaged in a life and death battle with animals, a custom popular in Rome at the time. Nobody had the right to abuse slaves and to exploit weak and poor people because all human beings were equal under the Christian God. Romans needed to stop using slaves in stadiums as a spectacle and needed to stop abusing slaves.

Roman authorities did not listen to the Christians and continued to persecute and kill many of them. Why did the Roman Empire fall? Roman citizens did not realize that Christians were the pioneers of a new era of the second kunmady, the man first era. The coming of man's era after the era of the nature gods has as its source natural causes which no human being can change. The Romans did not realize that the seasons changed and that they would need to change in order to adapt to the new season of humankind, the kunmady.

Man's era is one step in the natural course of human evolution, like nature's era, which is another step in the course of human evolution. If any person does not adjust to the natural change of the seasons, they must experience disadvantage, suffer, and maybe even die. Anybody who does not stop wearing a thick overcoat and thick boots in the summertime after wintertime and change to new clothes will have a difficult time surviving the intense heat. In the same way, Roman society, which is based on the slave system, had more slaves than citizens, and contradicted the new paradigm of man above all society. Naturally, Roman society collapsed because it did not adapt to the spirit of the times.

In America — a man above all society based on democracy, which is government for the people — there appeared a new kind of people. They believe that men and women are not the only children of God, and they believe that human beings are a part of nature. Humankind must stop conquering and destroying nature and will have to live with the rest of nature in harmony.

These people claim that nature also has an equal right to live on earth, and if nature disappears, human beings will disappear too. In other words, human beings must maintain a balanced and healthy relationship with nature in order to survive, otherwise, if there is no balance, then the air will become overpolluted, many of the natural species on the earth will die, and human beings, too, will become exinct. Some of these people are nature protectionists, naturalists, animal protectionists, scientists, and environmentalists. Like the early Christians in Rome, these people are pioneers of the next paradigm of Harmonism, a society which promotes a balanced relationship between human beings and the rest of the natural world. They give advice and even protest to the government and to major businesses to stop destroying nature and give everything in nature an equal right to survive. But the American government and major corporations do not listen to them and even callously throw them in jail, like Roman authorities who persecuted Christians for asking them to stop killing slaves in the stadium and to give Christians equal rights as human beings.

Rome, the greatest empire on the earth, eventually fell because the Romans did not follow the law of nature. If America, the strongest and richest nation on the earth, does not adjust to the new paradigm, then America will decline too. America must change government for only people to government for people and nature; otherwise, America will necessarily perish and fail to adapt to the new changes in the world.

Some people say that under democracy, which is government only for the people, we can still protect nature, but history proves the sheer impossibility of such a daunting task.

Aristocracy, which is government for only noble men, cannot protect the peasants. Governments based on slaves cannot protect slaves. The only way to protect peasants and slaves is to give them equal rights with the nobles and the slave owners.

In Rome, some people said they could have slaves as long as they treated slaves a little better. Actually, there were some people who treated slaves fairly and freed some of them.

Now, America has listed many species as being endangered and designed some areas that cannot be developed in order to protect nature, but that still has not succeeded and many of the endangered species of the earth are dying off as a result. In the same way, the only way to protect nature is to create a new political system in which nature can share the same rights to survive along with human beings. It is time to evolve from democracy, which is government only for the people, to Harmonism, which is government for both people and nature.

During the last 200 years in American history, American people faced a critical turning point — either Americans kept slavery or abolished it permanently. The black slave was treated as inferior to other human beings. The educated and civilized people in the North could not understand how human beings could oppress others and treat them like animals and remain civilized — the practice of slavery appalled them. Abolishing the slave system and the abuse of African Americans is a natural result of human evolution. After slavery was abolished, government for whites only changed to government for white and black people.

Because Lincoln had a vision for the future and was not willing to accept the degrading practice of slavery, he changed the course of human history. He had abolished slavery along with the belief that one race of human beings deserved to be treated as inferior. Lincoln had the courage and determination to change the backwards practice of slavery and reform society even though economists had told him that the economy would collapse if he ended the practice of slavery. Even though other politicians informed him people would resist change, he fought to emancipate African Americans from the terrible clutches of their masters. None of the plantation owners wanted to change society and were content with treating slaves as inferiors. They wanted to keep building their plantations and to expand their power, and they needed more slaves to do so.

Just like the America that needed a leader like Lincoln to change the course of human history and human evolution, the present-day America is sorely in need of a real change in the political system by a challenging and inspiring "leader."

* * * * * *

Now, during the final stage of vertical society, only the top people who are the most influential and who control other people below them are dominating the American people. In politics, small numbers of politicians influence and control all the political issues of the nation.

In economics, a small number of the wealthiest people almost control the American economy, and even much of the world economy.

This disturbing phenomenon is not only limited to economic and political matters; this trend has affected the sports world, movies, the fashion world, and cultural world. In every area, a very small number of stars dominate the entire field. For example, only a small number of sports stars are popular and powerful in the sports world. Only a few movie stars and directors predominate in the film industry.

But this unbalanced situation cannot last forever. Eventually, a society that has become so vertical must collapse. The people at the bottom, whose numbers have increased, will no longer be able to support the minority at the top, so the whole structure will eventually be demolished.

In the next century, when this vertical system turns into a horizontal system, then no small portion of people will dominate and oppress the majority of people. Everyone will have a fairly equal role and equal rights.

Since America is a democracy, which means government only for humankind, only those people who know the people well, who handle people well, and who take care of people well are in power.

Only those politicians who know what people want, who know how to get votes from people, who make gestures towards the people that the people like, and who make speeches that people like to listen to remain in power.

In the next century, in the information age, these people could not remain in power. Because most of them do not have much knowledge about the earth and nature, they will not be aware that this political issue — placing the earth first — will have priority over other concerns. Only those people with correct and precise information about both nature and people on earth and who have enthusiasm and love for people and nature will be in political power.

In democracy, any person who is eligible to vote can vote, even if he or she does not have any information about important political issues. Some people who even do not know the earth is spinning around the sun are still able to vote on world affairs. In the next century, in an information society, only those people who can use the computer and have full information and knowledge about the issue and the candidate can vote via the Internet. If a person cannot read, they cannot vote in this century. In the next century, people who will not be able to use the Internet will be disqualified from voting. In the future system, it will be very hard to mislead the majority of people with only good gestures and good speeches and without proper information. Political power will be fairly shared for those who vote with the Internet, and of course people will be able to vote at home.

Since the American economic system is free market capitalism, the people who have more money are naturally more powerful — the most influential people in American society now are at the top of mulitinational corporations.

Multinational corporations all over the world invest money, produce merchandise, and bring money and products to the American people. These corporations are similar to the Roman militia who destroyed small towns and villages, captured slaves, and brought them to Rome for the benefit of the Roman people.

American corporations are destroying nature all over the world and are bringing money and merchandise to America for the American people. In the next century, these destructive corporations will disappear, and the new corporations who will protect the earth and local people together — they will seek profit, but they would not do anything destructive of nature and local people, even if it is profitable. They will only do international business when the business will be in the interests of local people and nature; they will have to consult the local community whenever they conduct business in any given area.

Multinational corporations in the next century will not be like the Roman militia of antiquity; rather, they will be like the Peace Corps. The American Peace Corps project is a good beginning for the next century; it is a sign of the changing times. The Peace Corps philosophy will be the prime philosophy of the entrepreneurs who will do international business in the next century.

The environmental policy, nature protectionists, and animal protection philosophy will be changed. The term "environment" presently means a healthy environment for humankind and is based on an egocentric man-centered philosophy. The term "environmental protection" must be changed to "earth protection" because the earth is a mother of humankind and nature. Protecting the earth also protects humankind in the long run; environmentalists in the next century will not be working against human beings either, because they will consider human beings as children of the earth along with the rest of nature.

Now, America is promoting to the world democracy and human rights while the rights for nature to survive on earth are barely even acknowledged except by a few environmentalists and animal protectionists. Americans believe that they will last forever because America possesses a mighty military force that can destroy any enemy on earth, economic power that controls the entire world economy, and highly developed technology that can send spacecraft to Mars. Unless Americans protect nature and stop burning gas, the balance between the earth and humankind will grow hopelessly out of control with an increase in the global temperature by one percent. An increase in the average temperature of the earth by just one percent overall could cause the temperature in America to reach 20 degrees F higher than average and completely transform the climate. None of the military technology and economic power of America will be able to stop the forces of nature unleashed by the devastating change in climate. It will almost be impossible for humankind to survive because the fertile lands in America will turn into a desolate desert. On the edge of the desert, the Empire State Building will stand as a relic of a fallen civilization just like the ancient pyramids that are the only trace of ancient Egyptian civilization left for humankind.

Americans believe they will prosper forever, but they will not prosper without understanding the power and might of nature, which is mightier than any existing civilization. At the end of the twentieth century, the destructive forces on the earth are in power in America, but in the next century, the protective forces on the earth will be in charge in every area of American society if Americans desire a healthy future and take responsibility for their destiny.

ASIA

Many people say that the twenty-first century will be an Asian era, and most Asian people believe that they will develop into a superpower in the next century. Many Asian leaders use this idea as a slogan to promote their countries. Also, many academics in the West are convinced that Asia will play a significant role in the future.

These opinions stem from the rapid economic development in the Asian region, initiated by Japan, and the so-called four dragons, South Korea, Taiwan, Hong Kong, and Singapore. Now, there are the "new dragons": Thailand, Malaysia, Indonesia, and the Philippines. Most of all, the sudden emergence of China in international affairs, with magnificent economic development and an increase in military strength, and its influential role in international affairs, supports the idea of an emerging Asian era.

Even according to some media predictions concerning the status of Asia in the year 2030, one generation later, the Asian economy will be bigger than all other economies in the rest of the world. The collective military power in Asia will grow and become much more powerful than the United States military, and Asia will be capable of overpowering the Western nations, whether by armed force or through economic strength. Asia could control the entire world in the near future and become the center of the world. But we now know that is not possible with the recent collapse of the Asian economy, even though some economists predict a new upsurge in the Asian economy in the future.

Japan's GDP per capita has exceeded the United States' GDP per capita, and Malaysia has built the tallest skyscraper in the world. Korea has the largest Christian church in the world. Money, high-rise buildings, and churches are symbols of Western civilization that have become part of Asian culture.

Asia has already gained the capability to win the most important parts of Western civilization: money, Christianity, and high-rise buildings. If they possess other parts of Western culture, such as science, technology, culture, and military force, then it is naturally possible to believe that the center of modern civilization will move to Asia. Asia will therefore be a superpower of the world for the next century.

These predictions about the next century have made leaders in Western society quite nervous. In Western society, the fear of the legendary "yellow peril" is reviving, which evokes the memory of Genghis Khan, an Asian emporeror who paralyzed all Western people with fear. Frightened Western leaders are rushing to enforce NATO, an organization whose members are all from white nations — white people's nations are joining together to prepare for a future confrontation with yellow people's nations.

These opinions, predictions and fuss may be partially right, but they are basically wrong. This is another vision of the future with a locust mentality! These visions of the future do not take into account the paradigm shift, the change of religious doctrine, and the change of the political and economic system. These people believe that the vertical paradigm will never change, and the second God interpretation will never change. They feel that democracy and the free market economic system will last forever. They believe that if Asia becomes stronger and overpowers the West,

Asia will be the conqueror of the West and discriminate, humiliate, and exploit Western people. They believe that all Asian people believe in the Western God, Christianity, and they believe that almost every Asian person will have converted to Christianity in every corner of Asia, including in China, with a population 1.2 billion. Every town in Asia will have a Christian church.

They also believe that the Asian economy will keep growing, and the average annual income of Asian people will exceed American people's annual income sometime in the next century. There will be more high-rise buildings in most Asian cities that will be higher than in New York City.

The Asian population will expand to over five billion people sometime in the next century, and they will enjoy an American lifestyle, drive a car and have a large house, expensive clothes, and quality food as much as they want. If these predictions about the Asian era become true, there will be nothing left in nature. All nature will be destroyed, polluted, and not even a single tree will be left standing. If all nature disappears on earth, all Asian people will disappear, too, before they can enjoy the good life of the Asian era.

So, these scenarios which predict an Asian era have a basic flaw.

There might be an Asian era in the next century, and Asia could become the center of the world. But, the civilization of the Asian era will be totally different from the present era in Western civilization. If Asians want to be the center of the world, then they have to build a new civilization, instead of moving Western civilization into Asia.

Spring succeeds winter, but the paradigm of winter and spring are totally opposite. Winter's paradigm is cold; spring's paradigm is warm. Winter's symbols are snow and ice, and spring's symbols are bright flowers and butterflies. Flowers cannot be made from snow, nor can butterflies be made with ice.

In the same way, the Asian era, if it materializes, would not be made by the competence of Western civilization, such as high-rise buildings, Christian churches, and money. The new civilization, which might be built in an Asian era, will be totally different from present Western civilization — a contrast as remarkable as the difference between winter and spring.

The basic landscape will be totally changed, just like the melting snow that disappears and is replaced by colorful flowers. The landscape of both Western and Asian civilization will be totally transformed.

In order to find the right vision for the future, it is necessary to find out what the past has been like.

Asia has also experienced the first kunmady hunting age like all other civilizations. With the development of agrarian society, the second kunmady had started in Asia, the era of man first. In a short period of time, the founders of Taoism, Buddhism, and Confucianism appeared in Asia. Even though there are some differences between all of them, they all placed man above nature and believed that man had to be first like other religions in the second kunmady.

All these terms for Asian Gods, with Tien in Confucianism, Tao in Taoism, and Buddha in Buddhism, might appear different on the surface, but what they are talking about is the same since they are pioneers of the man first era. Like the Western Gods, their main purpose is to place man above all, but their conception of God is different. The other God is conceived by vision and hearing — the Western God made Moses hear the commandments and the Muslim God Allah talked to Mohammed through angels.

All the Asian Gods are not conceived by vision or hearing; they are conceived by human intuition. Buddha found God through enlightenment. Lao Tse did not say that he heard God, nor did Confucius. Words could not describe the character of God in Asian religion.

All of these Asian Gods are not even God from the Western perspective. However, the Asians Gods are still gods for man.

Nevertheless, they are not completely for man; they spared

some parts of their religion for nature. Taoism spared nature the most in Asian Gods. Lao Tse said, "Don't do anything artificially, just live naturally."

Buddha spared a large portion of nature, too. Buddha said, "Don't kill any animals; if you do, you will go to hell."

Confucianism is the most man centered belief in Asia. Confucius's God, Tien, is the image of man under the heavens on earth.

There is an interesting story in *The Analects of Confucius* that describes just how man centered Confucius' philosophy is.

One day, one disciple of Confucius rushed to Confucius and told him that there was a fire in a horse barn. Confucius asked if any people got hurt and did not ask if any animals were wounded. That shows how much a man centered thinker Confucius was.

Nevertheless, he also considered preserving nature. He preached that "a good man and a wise man should enjoy mountains and water." Basically, he believed that enjoying nature would be a significant part of the wise man's life.

All Asian Gods are Gods of man, but to a certain degree, they spared some portion of nature and a basic concept of living with nature in harmony.

In Asia, the second kunmady is also an era of conquering. In Asia, the stronger also conquered the weaker and maintained a vertical system. However, Asians did not totally wipe out and vanquish the weaker; all of the time, they considered the welfare interests of the weaker and the defeated.

Asians did not have a strong desire to conquer more and more; they compromised to a certain degree and harmonized with each other. Although the Chinese invented gunpowder, the compass, and martial arts, they did not have the ambition to conquer the whole world.

The basic belief and attitude of Asians are harmonizing with nature and other people to a certain degree. Because of this kind of belief and attitude, they were defeated by the Europeans, the believ- ers of the stronger man God and the strongest conqueror. After they were conquered, they found they had dropped behind the para- digm, and naturally, they wanted to catch up. In every area that Western people excelled in, they copied, followed, and learned from the West. In order to acquire the updated knowledge of the West, they needed to learn more and work more. They had to manufacture more, build more, and eventually they would have to destroy nature more and pollute the earth more. Now, in every major city in Asia, people can see more grimy smog and pollution than in any part of the world. In some cities, people can only breathe with masks because the air pollution is so thick.

It is hard to believe that the most polluted region in the world will be the center of the world in the next century.

If Asia wants to be the center of the world and create an Asia era, they have to clean the pollution and stop destroying the earth first.

* * * * * *

Another burden for Asia in the next century concerns the mounting tension and strife resulting from border conflicts.

India and Pakistan, China and Taiwan, North Korea and South Korea — these are the major border conflicts at the present time. These borders were designed by Western conquerors and are the consequence of Western occupation in Asia.

"Divide and rule" is the basic motto of conquerors.

As the winner of the era of the conqueror, America is handling very well these border confrontations and making a balance of power between each nation in order to keep Asian nations divided for American interests.

Because of borders, each nation is spending billions of dollars and a large portion of their national energy, in order to conquer their enemies, and now, most of them are developing or already have developed nuclear weapons. They are developing them in order to break down Western designed borders and conquer and unify with their enemies under their rule.

Under strict monitoring by the United States, they cannot use nuclear weapons or other weapons. Under the grip of the United States, there is no possible way for them to start a major war. Once the American grip is softened or the direction of American interests changes, it is quite possible these nations will get into a major war with nuclear weapons. It is very hard to imagine a potential nuclear disaster war zone as the center of world civilization.

If Asia wants to be the center of the world next century, they have to break down Western-made borders first and unify together, like the European Union.

But, Asian nations cannot break down those borders with guns and tanks unless the king of the world, America, says to do so. The only way they can break down those borders is by dumping all of the guns, tanks, and other weapons — mostly made in America and Europe - and with that money, build computers and give them to all of the people. Asian nations have to make Asian people meet with each other, talk to each other, and work together in cyberspace.

Then, Western-made borders will naturally disappear. Some Asian people, who believe that the Asian economy and military power will keep growing, and that someday, Asian nations will overpower the Western world, are definitely wrong. In the next century, winner and losers will not be determined by guns and money; rather, they will be determined by computers. People who believe they can conquer the world with guns and money are just like the Indian and African tribes that thought they could defeat the Europeans with bows and arrows.

Another problem Asians face is the loss of long-term vision. Since Asia started to imitate the West, Asian people have lost their beliefs and philosophy, and, most importantly, vision. To be a good follower, a man does not need a wide and long vision — all he has to do is look at the tail of the person he is following. Ever since Western nations controlled Asia, there has never been any single visionary who has a more advanced, wider, and creative vision for the future. In politics, economics, academic fields, science, and technology, no Asians have created new theories or new inventions for the world for over the last one hundred years. The most important inventions for human life, such as trains, automobiles, airplanes, telephones, and computers — none of them were invented by Asians. Influential political and economic theories, and even great art, have not been invented by Asians.

At the present time, every Asian nation is following Western ideology and copying Western political and economic systems. The left-wing ideas from the West — socialism and communism under a state-planned economic system — and the right-wing ideas of the West with capitalist free market economies are being implemented in Asia. Even culturally, militarily, and socially, Asians are interested in copying the West and, now, they are destroying nature in the same way as the West — in a frenzied rush for progress and material wealth. It seems likely that most Asians believe that all Asian customs, beliefs, arts, and systems are not important anymore, and everything that comes from the West is better than Asian culture. But they are wrong — Asia has a unique quality that is an improvement on the Western way of life. The most important skill for human beings in the real world is the ability to understand how the world is changing. Because Westerners are the winners of the man first era, the second kunmady, it is only natural that Westerners believe that man can do everything and can even change everything in the entire world. It is a textbook theory that human society changes because of class struggle in Western society. The members of the higher class exploit the lower class, and the lower class should eventually overthrow the higher class and free itself from the shackles of oppression. The working people are the lowest-class people in human society, and once the working people overthrow the capitalists, then there will be no existing lower classes. When communism materializes, people should be able to live a happy life, and there will be no need for revolution in the future since class contradictions will no longer exist. Communism should ideally last forever because it would be impossible for there to be any social problems in a classless society.

This Western theory sounds perfect, but this theory is based on the man first era mentality. After living about three thousand years in man's era, humankind became very arrogant and believed human beings could change all of society. There is no way this theory can fit the long-term vision for the next millennium - the third kunmady during which belief in the Third God will be the dominant interpretation of God's will.

For a long time, Asians have thought that the human world changes because of natural causes. Some Asian philosophers claimed that heaven changed the course of human existence. Asians were correct because the human world is changing as a result of a natural cause — evolution. Human beings can play a certain role in changing human society, but the basic changes must result from natural causes. In the next century, the idea that human beings can change everything will disappear; everyone will believe that human society changes because of natural causes.

There are some people who believe in communism under Asia.

Communism is basically a political system for working people only. Like aristocracy, which is a political system for nobles, communism is one step in the course of human evolution. From the perspective of the natural causes operating in human evolution, communism is one step above bourgeois society — there are more workers in the world than capitalists or bourgeois. But, communism is one step below democracy because American democracy uses all of the energy and the potential of its people to develop. American society includes nonworking people as well as working people and is naturally a larger society and more evolved than communism.

American democracy is the final stage of the human evolution of man's era — the second kunmady. After a long confrontation between the Americans and the Soviets, the Soviet Union collapsed, and there are many reasons that their economic system was bound to fail. Some people claim that the American technology and military system were better than the Soviet Union's system. They are partially right when they describe the collapse of the communist system and the development of a New World Order under the power of the United States. From the viewpoint of human history, it is quite natural that the Soviet Union lost the battle it was waging with America. American society is one step more evolved than the Soviet Union. American democracy is a broader political system than government only for the working people; people are much more open than under communism. Society is far more clear and transparent than in the former Soviet Union. Communism is an outdated system and designed by a man centered philosophy. If that is the case, why hasn't China collapsed? Many people wonder why, and they should understand that China is a country that was originally for peasants, not for workers. There are more peasants than workers in China, and China is a little more advanced than in the Soviet Union. The workers and the peasants in China are represented by the Chinese government. Most importantly, the most significant reason why China did not collapse along with its partner the Soviet Union and other communist nations arises from the fact that China opened up Hong Kong and its southern ports to the rest of the world. The Chinese government has gradually made their society more free and open to market forces than in the past.

There are many people in Asia that believe in democracy and the free market economy. Some Asian leaders claim that their GNP per capita will keep on climbing beyond $50,000 and with even surpass the GNP per capita in the United States. Some say that five billion people in Asia, including China and India, will be able to drive cars and enjoy a quality Western life in the next century. It is a fantastic, absurd, and practically insane idea to believe that this will be the case in the next century. As the sole superpower of the world, the world of the vertical paradigm, America will be more arrogant and selfish, and exploitative. America would not let Asian nations become rich and strong in order to someday challenge America. Asian nations have to live under the mercy of American corporations — it is a law of nature under the vertical system. Before, when the Americans competed with the Soviet Union for world hegemony, Americans helped Asian nations develop economically. But now, Americans who have become the sole superpower and control the whole world would not be so generous to Asian nations that want to keep developing economically. Even if Asian nations grow economically as much as they hope to in the future, the polarization between the rich and the poor is becoming wider and wider. Only a handful of Asians will take control of the economic system, and many grassroots people will become poorer and poorer. The way democracy functions is based on the philosophy "higher is better," and the free market economy is based on the philosophy "more is better." This is a vertical paradigm society; democracy and the free market economy are the most efficient and best systems under the vertical paradigm. As the vertical paradigm develops, rich nations will become richer, strong nations will become stronger, and the poor and weak nations will become poorer and weaker in the international world. The people will suffer the same inequalities — there will be more billionaires in Asia and more people suffering from poverty and even starving in Asia.

There will rise in Asia in the future a young generation who will not believe in democracy and capitalism, and they will not believe in socialism and communism. They will form the Third Force, neither right nor left wing. This younger generation will communicate with the Western progressive forces on the Internet, and they will cooperate with the younger generation in the West and take power from the Western followers, copycats, and admirers in Asia. They will break down Western-made borders and unify together all Asian nations and eventually all of the Western nations and the whole world.

When communist nations in the East bloc in Europe and capitalist nations in Western Europe confronted each other with NATO in the West and the Warsaw Pact in the East, they tried to develop hegemony in world affairs. Some politicians from Asia and Arab countries, as well as some nations in Europe, organized a group that they coined the "Third Force" which were neither allies with NATO nor with nations under the Warsaw Pact. They made a third group of nations that were separate from Western and communist nations and formed the Non-Alliance League. In their peak time, the membership of nations under this league was even more than one hundred, and many people believed they would create another important force in global affairs. Despite optimistic predictions about this newly created league, the Non-Alliance League unfortunately failed to achieve any concrete results.

They did not have a new ideology or a better system than the West bloc or the East bloc, and for this reason, they could not succeed. They tried to solve their problems with the social, political, and economic systems that were already in place in the West bloc and the East bloc — democracy or socialism. So, when the communist nations collapsed and the West bloc became the winner of global affairs, most of the Non-Alliance League nations all followed the West. Eventually, the Non-Alliance League developed an alliance with the West and completely vanished.

The new Third Force that will arise in Asia will be different from the old generation. The new generation will believe in the Third God, Harmonism, and the Earth Union, which are a one step more evolved ideology and system with which they can share with all of the younger generations in both the West and the East. They have one dream and one unified vision for the future, and they are a much more civilized generation than previous generations. They will deny all of the outdated ideologies and systems of the past, and they will want the whole world to develop and change.

The second kunmady is a man centered period in history and is the era of conquerors. Under the third kunmady, human beings and nature will make harmony. Asians are not as efficient in the conquest of nature as Western people, but harmonizing with nature and harmonizing rich and poor people is an activity that Asians are far more successful at than Western people. The era of conquering is now disappearing, and we will soon be entering the era of harmony. Harmony is a basic principle in Asian philosophy and a long lasting tradition, and if Asians stop the frenzied competition and destruction of nature along with the rest of the Western nations, if they protect nature and make a very harmonious relationship with it, then Asians will be the winners of the third kunmady. Asians will build a new civilization based on Harmonism, harmony between human beings and nature.

EARTHAN

Almost all people wonder whether the best system on earth, democracy, will become unfashionable in the next century and be replaced by a new system, Harmonism. They believe that democracy is the best system humankind has ever experienced and have difficulty imagining a different system. But what future will younger generations have to face unless there are some important changes made in the present vertical system? People who are aware of the problems we face coming into the next millennium will realize that there is no choice but to change the present system in order to ensure the survival of humankind and the natural world.

Throughout human history, people in the ruling classes have always believed that their system was the best and most advanced system possible — they believed their system would last forever and would be maintained by them forever. Pharaohs believed they would always remain in power, all the kings did, feudal lords did, the bourgeoisie did, and the communist politburo did, but eventually, all of their systems collapsed.

Now, in democracy, government for and by the people, all the people are rulers of nature (they can do virtually whatever they want to nature). They believe that democracy is the best system, and they want to maintain it and keep it forever. In the same way previous political systems collapsed, democracy must become outdated one day.

Because of the natural course of evolution, people's intelligence, common sense, and conscience cannot stand the old systems when they perceive its flaws, and then, they upgrade the system. When people become more intelligent and civilized, they cannot stand the slave system, so they abolish slavery and upgrade the system.

The younger generations who will live in the next century will be equipped with broad information from computers and the information age, and they will have a large, expansive vision for the future. They will collect all of the information happening on the earth immediately, and they will contact each other in every corner of the planet. They will not tolerate the polarization of the rich and the poor on the entire world — on one side of the earth, some people are dying from hunger, and on the other side, people are becoming too fat and spending millions of dollars on dieting. Naturally, they feel like equalizing the extreme difference between the rich and the poor. That is the beginning of a society based on Harmonism.

During human history, many conscientious and intelligent people did not like the huge difference between the rich and the poor, so they tried to improve society and create a more fair society. A fair and equal society has never materialized in spite of these people's diligent efforts.

Some ethnic people believe in living in harmony with nature — the American Indians, some Taoists who lived in mountains, the indigenous people of Australia, and some African people who believed in the nature gods. But strictly speaking, their society is not based on Harmonism with nature.

Harmonism must be based on information - without the correct information, there will be no possibility of harmonism. Harmonizing means leveling the gap between two different characters. In order to make harmony between man and nature, there must

194

be much information about both sides, nature and humankind — how nature functions, how human beings function and work, what nature needs or resists, what human beings desire or do not desire.

Even though human beings and nature are children of the earth, they have a totally different character. Human beings' character is destructive, while nature's character is productive. When human beings work, they destroy part of the earth in order to build civilization. Nature works to make the earth healthy and rich and has a different character than human beings.

Human beings cut down trees, build houses, eventually build huge buildings, dig in the earth, and build airplanes, ships, even space shuttles. In order to create, human beings want to build civilization and must destroy part of the earth in the process.

Nature creates and produces healthy trees, fresh air, and everything in nature occurs in cycles. One generation replaces the next generation and continues on into the future.

In the natural world, life is abundant in rain forests and in temperate forests with tall pine trees. In spring, all of nature blossoms and grows and the natural world flourishes. Nature's character is to make the earth healthy and rich, while the nature of human beings is destructive and often life destroying.

Humans destroy the earth, while nature develops the earth and makes it productive.

How can a balance be struck between a destructive and a productive character?

In order to make a good balance, we must have precise information about nature and humankind. How many trees does nature need in order to produce clean air? How many people can breathe healthily on earth and how many cars can be made without polluting the air too much? This balancing of the opposing characters of humans and nature requires precise information. In order to collect precise information about the delicate and complex natural world and the complicated world of human behavior and society, the human brain will not be enough — only computers can retain and process all of this vast information. Without computers, an accurate balance with nature is impossible. Harmonism could not be materialized without computers, like agrarian society could not materialize without the plow.

Ethnic people of primitive societies could not live in a harmonized society, even though many anthropologists and sociologists believe they did. They lived almost like an animal, as a part of the natural world.

With the computer, we can figure out how to reduce population, how many airplanes, cars, and other technology we can have, and still maintain a balance with nature. In other words, human beings can still build civilization, but because of accurate information from the computer, we will not exceed what the earth allows us to build.

* * * * * *

When will the new era of Harmonism start?

There are many people who believe in Harmonism as the only solution for the problems that human beings now confront. But many of them do not believe that Harmonism is realistic or will come soon in the near future — it will take a very long time for Harmonism to materialize on earth. According to them, Harmonism is against the free market economy, which only can survive by making more products, consuming more and spending more money, and developing more. The believers in the free market are so powerful and control the world now, so they would not do anything that would stop the free market system, even if, because of the free market system, all nature would eventually be destroyed and all humankind would die. Corporate executive officers are strong, and they control the world — everyone knows that.

Pharaohs were stronger than corporations, all kings were mightier than corporations, all noble men were more powerful than corporations, and even the Communist Party controlled their citizens more than corporations do. All of them are now gone. Corporations can control people, but they cannot control the law of great nature. Until they can stop the earth from spinning around the sun, no matter how strong they are, they have to follow the law of nature, or else they will disappear.

Harmonism is coming according to the law of great nature.

On earth, sometimes spring comes early, and sometimes spring comes late. Sometimes, spring comes in March, sometimes in April, and sometimes even in May. We cannot tell exactly when the paradigm and kunmady will change and bring Harmonism to the world — it is very hard to tell. If a person observes carefully when winter is almost over and the snow is already melting, small buds are already appearing under the sun, some birds are already migrating, and some animals are already coming out of hibernation.

In human society, there are already some people who believe that animals should have the same right to survive as human beings. Some people have stopped cutting trees and have maintained the forest from being developed. There are many people who claim that human beings should not contaminate the water or pollute the air with exhaust emissions. These animal rights activists, nature protectionists, and environmentalists are the pioneers of Harmonism. At the present time, these people try to achieve their goal in the existing political and economic system, democracy and the free market. Eventually, they will realize that under democracy, which is government only for the people, they cannot protect animals, nature, and the environment.

Before the French Revolution, some of the intelligent noble men tried to protect the peasants inside the aristocratic system, but they failed. Eventually, peasants were freed and protected only after the French Revolution. Before the American Civil War, there were also many conscientious and progressive American people who tried to protect slaves and sometimes, they helped the slaves gain freedom.

Nevertheless, they could not free all slaves until after the Civil War when the political system changed, and slavery was abolished. Now, there are many people all over the world who want to protect animals and nature, and someday, they will realize that under democracy, government only for the people, they cannot protect nature. They will realize that there must be a new political system that gives nature the same right to survive as human beings. Then, they will create a new system — Harmonism.

In order to practice Harmonism well, all the man-made borders of the two hundred nations will have to break down because animals and birds are moving around the earth, and contaminated water and polluted air flow and circulate while easily crossing over all the borders on the earth.

The potential development of biological and chemical weapons or other weapons of mass destruction must be monitored and inspected freely without any borders. In the next century, in order to live peacefully and maintain the earth clean, there must be a strong organization that can control the whole world and protect the earth — the Earth Union government.

People will believe that the earth will have a priority over their own national interest in the case of a conflict of interest. Protecting Mother Earth is every person's commitment. Many people in younger generations will imagine themselves as citizens of the earth — Earthans — instead of citizens of particular nations.

Harmonism and the Earth Union are around the corner — if this does not occur soon, the whole world will be in trouble. We have already disturbed the balance with nature. There is so much pollution all over the world, which proves that humankind pollutes more than nature can clean and restore.

There are still some people, mostly privileged and from older generations, who continue to believe in democracy and the free market economy. They believe and practice the ideals of consuming more and developing more, conquering nature, weaker people, and more market shares, and conserving all the money, property, and social status they already possess. These people who believe in conquering nature and weaker people will be called Condees. In order to maintain the existing system, these Condees will keep destroying nature and earth.

The Earthans who possess much information will find out about all the destruction that the Condees are creating. They will discuss with each other in cyberspace about how much destruction is occurring every day on the earth because of the Condees' greed and how much it is affecting human society along with the well-being of future generations. As the destruction by Condees persists, at a certain point, Earthans will realize that it is time for them to stand up in order to stop this frenzied destruction.

Naturally, there will form groups of people who want to destroy the earth and groups of people who protect the earth, and there will eventually be a confrontation between the Condees and the Earthans. Condees are mostly from the old generation, and Earthans are from the young generation.

There have been many confrontations in human society in history, such as tribe vs. tribe, ethnic vs. ethnic, and nation vs. nation, and all of these have led to war. The confrontation between Condees and Earthans is different. It is a confrontation, possibly even a war, between the people who destroy the earth and those who protect the earth. This confrontation will occur throughout the whole world because there is no nation on earth that is not affected by the struggle between the Condees and the Earthans. Regardless of nationality, gender, and ethnicity, people will be divided into two opposing sides — even some families will be divided. Even people from different religious backgrounds and from different places on the earth far away from one another will choose to side with either the Condees or the Earthans. Of course, there will be many bystanders who will not want to get involved and who don't care much about the earth and future generations of humankind and nature.

The war between Condees and Earthans will be carried out in a very civilized way because Earthans are the most evolved and civilized people on the earth. The war will start with Earthans passing information to Condees that shows how imminent the destruction of the earth is at the present time unless changes are made, and they will educate the Condees about the basic character of humankind and nature — there must be a balance between humans and nature. They will reveal the magnificent strength of the laws of nature and will show them that anyone who goes against the laws of nature must eventually be destroyed.

Some Condees will listen and understand, and eventually, they will compromise with the Earthans or even join them. Still, the staunch Condees will continue to destroy the earth and make more money. Earthans will start to protest on the sites of destruction and pollution by the Condees in order to stop the incessant destruction and contamination of the earth.

After this stage, Earthans all over will use the skill and technology and sabotage the destructive businesses and projects of the Condees.

Most of the Condees will not stand with their arms crossed and be idle — that's not the character of Condees. Throughout human history, the Condees did not listen to the young and progressive generations; instead, they oppressed and persecuted young generations who bravely tried to create a better society.

In most cases when the political system was changing into a new system, the older generations depended on guns and money in order to defeat the younger generations. King Louis in France possessed lots of gold and enough guns to kill his citizens, and Tsar Nicholas in Russia had one of the largest armies on all of the earth and had more than ten tons of gold — but these guns and gold couldn't stop the people from changing the outmoded old society to a new and improved society.

This time, Condees will act the same way even though this

strategy failed numerous times before. They might strengthen their military forces to destroy Earthans. They might collect a huge amount of money to block the Earthans' activity. However, their strategy might not work because war in the next century is not like conventional warfare, which uses guns, tanks, and missiles. It will be an information war, and Earthans and Condees will not fight in a battlefield — they will fight in cyberspace. So, Condees cannot locate their enemies easily — they cannot find any target to shoot at or bomb or destroy their enemies. Earthans will not use any weapons; they will only depend on information technology and will fight with information technology. With computers, they will be able to stop the Condees' operation — warships, airplanes, and tanks.

It is hard to tell if the confrontation between the Earthans and the Condees will develop into a cold war and finally a hot war. A decade ago, when communism and democracy confronted each other, many people worried about the cold war developing into a hot war during which both sides would use all of the nuclear weapons at their disposal and destroy each other along with most people on the earth. The highly developed intelligence of modern people prevented them from unleashing massive weapons of nuclear and chemical destruction and destroying the earth. So, the earth war will not develop into a hot war or even a cold war.

Earthans are a civilized and informed people, and they will avoid the tragic consequences of a heated confrontation with the Condees. They will act very peacefully towards the Condees.

There will be a big natural catastrophe caused by the Condees' constant destruction of nature — such as the future consequences of global warming, or floods, or melting of the ice caps. Catastrophic diseases and epidemics caused by polluted air and water will also kill many people, which will push the Condees into a corner. Then, there will be a great leader, like Lincoln, who will dedicate his whole life to changing society and will have courage and a unique vision for the future. With his leadership, the last staunchiest Condees will be defeated, and people will formally agree under the new political system of Harmonism that nature has an equal right to survive along with humankind.

All the leaders of the world will organize the Earth Union to ensure the protection of the earth and humankind for future generations.

The first major project of the Earth Union government will be a major cleanup of the earth and the restoration of damaged nature will occur. All of the people on earth will participate directly and indirectly in this large project in human history. New technology and new inventions will be created, and there will be millions of new jobs which will be created to clean up the earth and restore nature. The population will be controlled, and the differences between rich and poor harmonized. Every field will be updated to meet the demands of the new paradigm.

In Harmonism, the Earth Union people will be more peaceful, more free, more friendly, and more open. There will be no conquering of nature, nor will other stronger men conquer weaker men and women. Under Harmonism, conquering will be against harmonism. The vertical paradigm will collapse and everyone will have equal rights.

Even though there is no conqueror, there will still be differences between people. There will be more arguments under Harmonism because people will have to discuss their views and make a balance.

Especially, the representatives of human beings in Congress and the representatives of nature will constantly argue and disagree with one another in order to make a balance between man and nature. The human side will want more development, more land, and more materials. They will want to build more factories and develop more industries and buildings and will keep asking to develop more. The representatives of nature will be very stingy about nature and will not easily forsake nature for man's welfare in order to protect nature; they will want forests to expand and grow, along with more national parks, and more wildlife areas.

After cleaning up the earth, then, we will build a new civilization based on Harmonism with new constructions and designs for houses and cities. The landscape will change and become much more beautiful — cities without pollution will be built.

The next most important project will be the exploration of space in order to find another planet where human beings can live. All of human energy and technology will be used to travel into space once Harmonism is established on earth.

The twentieth century will be the last stage of the vertical paradigm, the end of man's God, the final period of the second kunmady, and the end of the era of the conqueror.

The twenty-first century will inaugurate the beginning of the horizontal paradigm, the beginning of the Third God, and the beginning of the era of harmonizing — a century for Earthans.

EDITOR'S NOTE

This is an edited transcription from Teacher So Namoo concerning what will happen in the future.

People come to the Teacher whenever they have questions and problems.

Teacher seldoms says no if the students have a question, and he answers, explains and teaches about whatever people ask.

He doesn't have a textbook when he teaches because his teachings do not address issues discussed in textbooks.

He doesn't have a classroom, and any place he goes to becomes a classroom.

He never claims that what he teaches and what he talks about is the truth.

Some people say he is a crazy man. Some people say he is a wise man.

Some people may believe what he teaches is the truth.

SOME NOTES ABOUT
THE MANUSCRIPT

First, there are no proper words in the English vocabulary to describe some of the words used in this text such as kunmady. Second, Teacher wished to present his ideas in a clear manner that is accessible to everyone, even a tenth grade audience. He wants the message in this book to reach the younger generation as well as the older generation; he wants to spread his message across the world. His ideas are so radical and the presentation of his ideas occurred in a very choppy, elliptic style because he wished the reader to think about the controversial ideas in this book. I avoided writing in a fancy style in order to maintain the simple yet profound style of Teacher's words; I also wanted to avoid writing sentences that would appear pretentious rather than humble. I wanted to preserve Teacher So Namoo's uniquely Asian style in the presentation of his ideas, in order to preserve the rhythm and authenticity of his discourse. His thoughts are very profound, and I suggest that readers take time to consider them and learn from them. Many other people contributed to the editing and dictation of this manuscript in the past, but I personally took on the responsibility of editing the dictation of the final manuscript as a Ph.D. in Comparative Literature.

— The Editor, Dr. Raphael Comprone, Ph.D.